Punchline
QUOTABLE QUOTES

Naresh Chandra Mathur

PUSTAK MAHAL®

Publishers
Pustak Mahal®
J-3/16 , Daryaganj, New Delhi-110002
☎ 23276539, 23272783, 23272784 • *Fax:* 011-23260518
E-mail: info@pustakmahal.com • *Website:* www.pustakmahal.com

Branches
Bengaluru: ☎ 080-22234025 • *Telefax:* 080-22240209
E-mail: pustak@airtelmail.in • pustak@sancharnet.in
Mumbai: ☎ 022-22010941, 022-22053387
E-mail: rapidex@bom5.vsnl.net.in
Patna: ☎ 0612-3294193 • *Telefax:* 0612-2302719
E-mail: rapidexptn@rediffmail.com

ISBN 978-81-223-1247-8

Edition: 2012

Printed at : Sharma Printers, Delhi

Extracts from Reviews

- (With Prayer)

  – Rev. His Holiness Spiritual Guru and Nobel Laureate,
  Dalai Lama.

- The Punchline is very interesting and it was with me during a 4-week stay in Italy. It helped me a great deal. You have choosen the quotes with great human insight.

  – Tara Gandhi Bhattacharjee
  Vice Chairperson, Gandhi Smriti and Darshan Smriti, New Delhi

- 'Punchline' explains Mathur's penchant to pursue cancer as his way of service to the world.

  – Hindustan Times, Patna, Wednesday, December 7, 2011

- Thanks for the wonderful book on Quotable Quotes. While it offerred great quotations, it was pleasure to find contemporary axioms. Moreover the drive against cancer was very educative.

  – Counsellor Cell: High Commission for Pakistan, New Delhi
  Muhammad Shafique-ur-Rehman

- This is a good book. I wish you all the best for your cancer awareness campaign.

  – Sushil Kumar, KBC 5 Jackpot Winner of Rs. 5 crore

The Three Wise Monkeys are a pictorial maxim. Together they embody the proverbial principle to "see no evil, hear no evil, speak no evil". Sometimes there is a fourth monkey depicted with the three others; the last one, symbolises the principle of "do no evil". He may be shown crossing his arms.

"Tobacco smokers become callous and careless of others' feelings... probably tobacco kills the finer feelings... the smoker fills his house with smoke, the chewer dirties every corner and the snuffer his clothes."

– Mahatma Gandhi

PREFACE

A small step:
Na Umra Ki Seema Ho...

When I got the incredible news for publication of my maiden book *Punchline* by a reputed publisher, **M/s Pustak Mahal**. I was just jumping, thumping and what not I retired as Assistant General Manager from State Bank of India, Patna on 31st January 2011. In my farewell, our Chief General Manager, Shri Jeevandas Narayan blesssed me that "You have played a glorious inning and the second inning will be more beautiful". It is true to me. Courtesy Pustak Mahal.

I express thanks for extending 365 x 24 support for typing, photostat and internet working by Shri Dhirendra Guru and team, Shri Manish Sinha for designing and Shri Rehan, Shri Naseem Ahmed for shaping the book at initial stage. I remiss in not mentioning the name of Shri Vijay Bahadur Singh, family friend who shoulder the responsibility of microscopic checking. Shri C.P. Jain, born in SBI together and Shri M.R. Rahman, Branch Manager, Pustak Mahal, Patna both have appreciated and encouraged all along.

Back to my nest, my wife Smt Kalpna Mathur at least spared me from domestic work that too post retirement when my sensex U-turned abruptly for fulfilment of my mission. My both sons Ankit Mathur (Edinburgh-UK) and Anchit Mathur (DU student) all the time peeped my progress of *Punchline* with suppressed, oppressed, compressed and depressed smile now turn into burst of laughter. In loving memory, I dedicate this book to my parents Late J.P. Mathur & Late Savitri Mathur.

I have made every attempt to make the book enjoyable. However, bugs and cracks are always possible. I regret the shortcoming. *Punchline* is different from Quote Books. Is it not! Hold it firmly! Open it gently! Turn any page to continue... You will have pearl every time. The ultimate – the voice of the reader is the voice of the God. My will is Almighty and Almighty is my will. I am dead eager to discover how much you liked my book "Punchline". So, please don't forget to drop me a e-mail.

Namaste Mathur,

Naresh Chandra Mathur
Nala Road, Petrol Pump, Anupama Apartment,
Flat No. 2-A, Near Dr. P.K. Mukherjee,
Patna – 800004 (Bihar)
Mob.: 09955115542 & LL 0612-2721604
Email: nareshchandramathur@gmail.com

Well Said

PEARLS OF WISDOM

- A bank is a place that will lend you money if you can prove that you don't need it.

  – Bob Hope

- A borderless society with no divisions of caste and community can only rise from borderless minds.

  – A.P.J. Abdul Kalam

- A champion is afraid of losing. Everyone else is afraid of winning.

  – Bilie Jean King

- A comfortable old age is the reward of a well-spent youth.

  – Maurice Chevalier

- A joke is a very serious thing.

  – Winston Churchill

- A laugh is a smile that bursts.

  – Mary H. Waldrip

- A law is valuable not because it is law but there is right in it.

  – H.W. Beecher

- A lie has no leg, but a scandal has wings.

  – Thomas Fuller

- A lie has no legs. It has to be supported by thousand other lies. One has to memorise all

Cancer can not conquer my spirit.

these lies without break in chain, whereas honesty does not need as such.

– John Mason

- A little learning is a dangerous thing.

  – Alexander Pope

- A man can get a reputation from very small things.

  – Sophocles

- A man never becomes an orator if he has anything to say.

  – Finley Peter Dunne

- A man who stands for nothing will fall for anything.

  – Malcolm X

- A mind always employed is always happy. This is the true secret, the grand recipe, for felicity.

  – Thomas Jefferson

- A proverb is a short sentence based on long experience.

  – Miguel De Cervantes

- A real friend is one who walks in when other walks out.

  – Swami Chinmayananda

- A smile is the universal welcome.

  – Max Eastman

- A value is a value for me only when I see the value of the value as valuable to me.

  – Swami Dayanand

- A woman is one who shows a man what love, sharing and caring is all about. That is the essence of a woman.

  – Sushmita Sen

Tobacco in all forms is injurious.

- After darkness, the sun rises – and it always rises in the east.

  – Peter Velappan

- Age is no guarantee of maturity.

  – Lawana Blackwell

- All books are divisible into two classes, the books of the hour and the books of all times.

  – John Ruskin

- All the mistakes I have ever made were when I wanted to say 'No' and said 'Yes'.

  – Moss Hart

- A room without books is like a body without a soul.

  – Marcus Tullius Cicero

- All work, even cotton spinning, is noble, work alone is noble.

  – Thomas Carlyle

- An artist is not paid for his labour but for his vision.

  – James Whistler

- At twenty one, she lived in a one-room flat over her father's grocery shop and dreamed of public service.

  – Margaret Thatcher

- Attitude is everything.

  – Diane Von Furstenberg

- Be hungry for success.

  – Og Mandino

- Be kind whenever possible. It is always possible.

  – Dalai Lama

I exercise, I do not smoke!

- Before I got married, I had six theories about bringing up children, now I have six children and no theories.

  – John Wilmot

- Better mad with the rest of the world than wise alone.

  – Baltasar Gracian

- Be wisely worldly, but not worldly wise.

  – Francis Quarles

- Bhutan GDP is "Gross National Happiness". I care less about the Gross National Product and more about the Gross National Happiness.

  – Jigme Singye Wangchuk

- Chaotic action is preferable to orderly inaction.

  – Will Rogers

- Children have neither a past nor a future. Thus they enjoy the present, which seldom happens to us.

  – Jean de la Bruyere

- Children have to be educated, but they have also to be left to educate themselves.

  – Ernest Dimnet

- Circumstances have changed us, and we have changed circumstances.

  -Atal Behari Vajpayee

- Circumstances rule men and not men rule circumstances.

  – Euripides

- Citizenship consists in the service of country.

  – Jawaharlal Nehru

Smoking is bad for the health.

- 'Classic', a book which people praise and don't read.

  – Mark Twain

- Come live in my heart, and pay no rent.

  – Samuel Lover

- Credit Card : A way of saying buy-buy to your money.

  – Jug Suraiya

- Criminals do not die by the hands of the law. They die by the hands of other men.

  – George Bernard Shaw

- Customs are more powerful than laws.

  – The Talmud

- Delay is preferable to error.

  – Thomas Jefferson

- Do it or don't do it, but never maybe do it.

  – Tristan Loo

- Do not read beauty magazines. They only make you feel ugly.

  – Mary Schmich

- Do or do not, there is no try.

  – George Lucas

- Do we not live in dreams?

  – Alfred Lord Tennyson

- Do your work with your whole heart, and you will succeed – there is so little competition.

  – Elbert Hubbard

- Don't stop at the top, touch the sky before you drop.

  – Scorpions

Tobacco lovers – Enemy of society.

- Don't worry about your heart, it will last you as long as you live.

– W.C. Fields

- Dream as if you will live forever. Live as if you will die today.

– James Dean

- Each success only buys an admission ticket to a more difficult problem.

– Henry Kissinger

- Eat breakfast like a king, lunch like a prince, and dinner like a pauper.

– Adelle Davis

- Education commences at the mother's knee and every word spoken within the hearing of little children tends towards the formation of character.

– Hosea Ballou

- Education must lead to be creation of job providers rather than job seekers.

– A.P.J. Abdul Kalam

- Enthusiasm moves the world.

– Arthur Balfour

- Everbody wants to do something to help, but nobody wants to be first.

– Pearl Bailey

- Every child is an artist. The problem is how to remain an artist once he grows up.

– Pablo Picasso

- Every man desires to live long, yet no man desires to be old.

– Jonathan Swift

Tobacco is the way to die,
so don't buy and say it good bye.

- Every portrait that is painted with feeling is a portrait of the artist, not of the sitter.

  – Oscar Wilde

- Every really new idea looks crazy at first.

  – Abraham H. Maslow

- Every winner has scars.

  – Herbert N. Casson

- Everybody hates me because I'm so universally liked.

  – Peter De Vries

- Everybody is ignorant, only on different subjects.

  – Will Rogers

- Everybody wants to go to heaven, but nobody wants to die.

  – Joe Louis

- Everyone loves to be loved.

  – Mark Spitz

- Everyone thinks of changing the world, but no one thinks of changing himself.

  – Leo Tolstoy

- Everything has its beauty, but not everyone sees it.

  – Confucius

- Everywhere is within walking distance if you have the time.

  – Steven Wright

- Example is not the main thing in influencing others, it is the only thing.

  – Albert Schweitzer

Cancer never takes vacation.

- Faith: Not wanting to know what is true.

  – Friedrich Nietzsche

- Fatigue is the best pillow.

  – Benjamin Franklin

- Fear does not exist anywhere except in the mind.

  – Dale Carnegie

- Fighting fire with fire only gets you ashes!

  – Abigail Van Buren

- Follow your dream.

  – Kalpana Chawla

- Food is an important part of a balanced diet.

  – Fran Lebowitz

- Football: If you are first, you are first. If you are second, you are nothing.

  – Bill Shankly

- For every action there is an equal and opposite government programme.

  – Bob Wells

- For all, life is a dream, and dreams themselves are only dreams.

  – Pedro Calderon de la Barca

- For every disciplined effort there is a multiple reward.

  – Jim Rohn

- Force overcome by force.

  – Cicero

- Forgive your enemies, but never forget their names.

  – John F Kennedy

Avoid tobacco, avoid cancer.

- Get your facts first, and then you can distort them as much as you please.

  – Mark Twain

- God does not play dice with the universe.

  – Albert Einstein

- God is a circle, whose centre is everywhere and circumference nowhere.

  – Voltaire

- God will forgive me. It's his job.

  – Heinrich Heine

- Good judgment comes from experience, and experience comes from bad judgment.

  – Barry LePatner

- Good laws have their origins in bad morals.

  – Ambrosius Macrobius

- Good taste is better than bad taste, but bad taste is better than no taste.

  – Arnold Bennett

- Government does not solve problems, it subsidises them.

  – Ronald Reagan

- Growing old is not so much of a problem as the fear of being old.

  – Dr. Theodore R.Van Dellen

- Habit, if not resisted, soon becomes necessity.

  – St. Augustine

- Half the world is composed of people who have something to say and cannot, and the other half who have nothing to say and keep on saying it.

  – Robert Frost

If you smoke yourself – you must practice what you preach.

- Happiness is the interval between periods of unhappiness.

  – Don Marquis

- Having a wife is part of Living. But having girl friend along with wife is Art of Living.

  – Sri Sri Ravi Shankar

- Having nothing, nothing can he lose.

  – William Shakespeare

- He who flees will fight again.

  – Tertullian

- He who moves not forward, goes backward.

  – Johann Wolfgang von Goethe

- He who trusts secrets to a servant, makes him his master.

  – John Dryden

- Honesty is the first chapter in the book of wisdom.

  – Thomas Jefferson

- Hope never abandons you, you abandon it.

  – George Weinberg

- How much money is enough money? "Just a little bit more."

  – John D. Rockfeller

- How wonderful it is that nobody need to wait a single moment before starting to improve the world.

  – Anne Frank

- I always advise people never to give advice.

  – P.G. Wodehouse

Papa! Make tobacco free family.

- I am at peace with God. My conflict is with man.

  – Charlie Chaplin

- I am serious when I do my work. I am not serious when I am with my kids.

  – Bill Gates

- I am the master of my fate. I am the captain of my soul.

  – William Ernest Henley

- I can, therefore I am.

  – Simone Weil

- I don't know who invented high heels, but all women owe him a lot.

  – Marilyn Monroe

- I feel so miserable without you, it's almost like having you here.

  – Stephen Bishop

- I would rather do and not promise than promise and not do.

  – Arthur Warwick

- I have come to the conclusion that politics is too serious a matter to be left to the politicians.

  – Charles de Gaulle

- I have had many troubles in my life, but the worst of them never came.

  – James A Garfield

- I have made this letter longer than usual, only because I have not had the time to make it shorter.

  – Blaise Pascal

- I hear and I forget. I see and I remember. I do and I understand.

  – Confucius

Tobacco or health : Choose health.

- I keep six honest serving men. They taught me all I knew, their names are WHAT, WHY, WHEN, HOW, WHERE and WHO. It can teach you to get brilliant ideas.

  – Rudyard Kipling

- I speak two languages, Body and English.

  – Mae West

- I use the rules to frustrate the law. But I didn't set up the ground rules.

  – F.Lee Bailey

- I was seldom able to see an opportunity until it had ceased to be one.

  – Mark Twain

- If a man be gracious and courteous to strangers, it shows he is a citizen of the world.

  – Francis Bacon

- If a man will begin with certainties, he shall end in doubts, but if he will content to begin with doubts, he shall end in certainties.

  – Francis Bacon

- If poverty is the mother of crime, lack of good sense is the father of them.

  – Jeande la Bruyere

- If there is a will, prosperity can't be far behind.

  – W.C. Fields

- If we all are reasonable, law will be superfluous.

  – Baruch Spinoza

- If we could sell our experiences for what they cost us, we'd all be millionaires.

  – Abigail Van Burren

Smoking – The horrible habit that invites premature death!

- If you can find something everyone agrees on, it's wrong.

– Mo Udall

- If you cannot convince them, confuse them.

– Harry S Truman

- If you cannot do great things, do small things in a great way.

– Napoleon Hill

- If you choose not to decide, you still have made a choice.

– Neil Peart

- If you do not conquer self, you will be conquered by self.

– Napoleon Hill

- If you do not like something, change it, if you can not change it, change your attitude. Do not complain.

– Maya Angelou

- If you have a problem with my answer that's your problem, not mine.

– Dennis Rodman

- If you have integrity, nothing else matters. If you don't' have integrity, nothing else matters.

-Alan K. Simpson

- If you judge people, you have no time to love them.

– Mother Teresa

- If you keep rephrasing the question, it gradually becomes the answer.

– Robert Brault

Cancer is not a death warrant.
Only awareness is protection.

- If you lack faith, you will have to pray for it. But to pray, you need faith. That is the paradox.

– Sri Sri Ravi Shankar

- If you remain soft then more and more burden will be loaded on your shoulders.

– Quotes of Sardar Patel

- If you risk nothing, then you risk everything.

– Geena Davis

- If you see a snake, just kill it – Don't appoint a committee on snakes.

– Ross Perot

- If you talk to a man in a language he understands, that goes to his head. If you talk to him in his language, that goes to his heart.

– Nelson Mandela

- If you think you can do a thing or think you cannot do a thing you are right.

– Henry Ford

- If you want something said, ask a man, if you want something done, ask a woman.

– Margaret Thatcher

- If you want to catch something, running after it is not always the best way.

– Lois McMaster Bujold

- Improvement begins with I.

– Arnold H.Glasow

- In about the same degree as you are helpful, you will be happy.

– Karl Reiland

- In charity there is no excess.

– Francis Bacon

Zindagi hoti hai sabse khas,
tambakoo ko na aane do pass.

- In film, you are a totally different person than in the video.

– Aaliah, Musician

- In quarreling the truth is always lost.

– Publilius Syrus

- Incompetents invariably make trouble for people other than themselves.

– Larry McMurtry

- It is a thousand times better to have common sense without education than to have education without common sense.

– Robert Green Ingersoll

- It is always death that comes before your desires are fulfilled. Even if you live for a thousand years, your desires are not going to be fulfilled.

– Osho Quets on Death

- It is always the best policy to speak the truth, unless, of course, you are an exceptionally good liar.

– Jerome K. Jerome

- It is better to be faithful than famous.

– Theodore Roosevelt

- It is better to light one small candle than to curse the darkness.

– Confucius

- It is better to travel than to arrive.

– Buddha

- It is certain because it is impossible. It is certain because it is possible.

– Tertullian

Give cancer the boot.

- It is not death, but dying, which is terrible.

  – Henry Fielding

- It is not that successful people are givers, it is that givers are successful people.

  – Patti Thor

- It is often easier to ask for forgiveness than to ask for permission.

  – Grace Murray Hopper

- It is the dull man who is always sure, and the sure man who is always dull.

  – H.L. Mencken

- It is the greatest of all mistakes to do nothing because you can only do little – do what you can.

  – Sydney Smith

- It is twice the pleasure to deceive the deceiver.

  – Jean Dela Fontaine

- It's easier to run for office than to run the office.

  – Thomas P. O'Neill

- It matters more how one gives than what one gives.

  – Pierre Corneille

- John Milton, the poet when he got married, he wrote "Paradise Lost". When his wife died, he wrote "Paradise Regained".

  – John Milton

- Keep your face to the sunshine and you cannot see the shadow.

  – Helen Keller

- Keeping calm under severe pressure and self-belief conquered all.

  – Gautam Ghambir, World Cup Final Victory (2011)

Cancer is not contagious.

- Kites rise highest against the wind, not with it.

  – Winston Churchill

- Knowledge is not information, it's transformation.

  – Osho Quotes

- Laugh until it helps!

  – Laugh Club Motto

- Laws grind the poor, and rich men rule the law.

  – Oliver Goldsmith

- Laziness may appear attractive, but work gives satisfaction.

  – Anne Frank

- Leadership is action, not position.

  – Donald H. McGannon

- Learn the fundamentals of the game and stick to them. Band-Aid remedies never last.

  – Jack Nicklaus

- Life: If you rest, you rust.

  – Helen Hayes

- Life is wide, limitless. There is no border, no frontier.

  – Bruce Lee

- Light is the symbol of truth.

  – James Russell Lowell

- Life shrinks or expands in proportion to one's courage.

  – Anais Nin

From a moral point of view, smoking is a deliberate act of self destruction.

- Listening is very inexpensive, not listening could be very costly.

– Tom Brewer

- Logic will get you from A to B. Imagination will take you everywhere.

– Albert Einstein

- Long range planning works best in the short term.

– Doug Evelyn

- Love, the quest, marriage, the conquest, divorce, the inquest.

– Helen Rowland

- Love that is not madness, is not love.

– Pedro Calderon de la Barca

- Lying can never save us from another lie.

– Vaclav Havel

- Make money your God and it will plague you like the devil.

– Henry Fielding

- Make sure you have finished speaking before your audience has finished listening.

– Dorothy Sarnoff

- Make your smile cheaper, and your anger expensive.

– Sri Sri Ravi Shankar

- Man is born free, and everywhere he is in shackles.

– Jean Jacques Rousseau

Cancer is not just a horoscope sign but the right test can foretell your future.

- Man is by nature a political animal.

  – Aristotle

- Man was made at the end of the week's work when God was tired.

  – Mark Twain

- Many a treasure besides Ali Baba's is unlocked with a verbal key.

  – Henry Van Dyke

- Men seldom make passes at girls who wear glasses.

  – Dorothy Parker

- Men try to run life according to their wishes; life runs itself according to necessity.

  – Jean Toomer

- Money is like a sixth sense without which you cannot make a complete use of the other five.

  – W. Somerset Maugham

- Money is not everything but it surely keeps you in touch with your children.

  – J. Paul Getty

- Money is not everything, but everything is money.

  – The Boring Dekan

- Money often costs too much.

  – Ralph Waldo Emerson

- Mothers all want their sons to grow up to be president, but they don't want them to become politicians in the process.

  – John Fitzgerald Kennedy

Cervix cancer is a leading cause of death.

- My mistakes are my life.

  – Samuel Beckett

- My toughest fight was with my first wife.

  – Muhammad Ali

- Nature can do more than physicians.

  – Oliver Cromwell

- Nature soaks every evil with either fear or shame.

  – Tertullian

- Never interrupt your enemy when he is making a mistake.

  – Napoleon Bonaparte

- Never look where you are going. Always look where you want to go.

  – Bob Ernst

- Never play a thing in the same way twice.

  – Louis Armstrong

- Never teach your child to be cunning for you may be certain that you will be one of the first victims of his shrewdness.

  – Josh Billings

- Never tell everything at once.

  – Ken Venturi

- Never turn down a job because you think it is too small, you do not know where it can lead.

  – Julia Morgan

- 'No comment' is a splendid expression. I am using it again and again.

  – Winston Churchill

Cancer is a word, not a sentence.

- No man can be happy without a friend nor be sure of his friend till he is unhappy.

  – Osho Quotes

- No man is above the law and no man is below it; nor do we ask any man's permission when we ask him to obey it.

  – Theodore Roosevelt

- No man is rich enough to buy back his past.

  – Oscar Wilde

- No man stands so straight as and when he stoops to help a boy.

  – Knights of Pythagoras

- No nation has friends only interests.

  – Charles de Gaulle

- No one can make you feel inferior without our consent.

  – Eleanor Roosevelt

- No one has ever become poor by giving.

  – Anne Frank

- No person was ever honoured for what he received. Honour has been the reward for what he gave.

  – Calvin Coolidge

- No pressure, no diamonds.

  – Mary Case

- Nobody ever died of laughter.

  – Max Beerbohm

- Nobody likes the man who brings bad news.

  – Sophocles

- Not only strike while the iron is hot, but make it hot by striking.

  – Oliver Cromwell

Eat right, be bright.

- Not truth, but faith, it is that keeps the world alive.

  – Edna St Vincent Millay

- Nothing can be beautiful which is not true.

  – John Ruskin

- Nothing exceeds like excess.

  – Al Jourgensen

- Nothing happens unless first we dream.

  – Carl Sandburg

- Nothing is beautiful from every point of view.

  – Horace

- Nothing is impossible, the word itself says "I m possible."

  – Audrey Hepburn

- Nothing is said that has not been said before.

  – Terence

- Nothing recedes like success.

  – Walter Winchell

- Nothing succeeds like success.

  – Alexandre Dumas

- Nowadays anyone, who cannot speak English and is incapable of using the Internet is regarded as backward.

  – Al Waleed bin Talal

- Nowadays selfishness is no monopoly of one class but has been more or less socialised.

  – Paul Brunton

- Obviously crime pays, or there'd be no crime.

  – G. Gorden Liddy

Extend support for treatment and psychological care to cancer patients.

- Once you choose hope, anything is possible.

  – Christopher Reeve

- Once you start buying first-aid kits, you start having accidents.

  – George Mikes

- One death is a tragedy, one million is a statistic.

  – Joseph Stalin

- One enemy is too much. Thousand friends are not enough.

  – George Herbert

- One machine can do the work of fifty ordinary men. No machine can do the work of one extraordinary man.

  – Elbert Hubbard

- One is often guilty by being too just.

  – Pierre Corneille

- One man with courage is a majority.

  – Thomas Jefferson

- One today is worth two tomorrows.

  – Benjamin Franklin

- One with God is a majority.

  – Billy Graham

- Only strength respects strength.

  – A.P.J. Abdul Kalam

- Opportunity makes a thief.

  – Francis Bacon

- Our school education ignores, in a thousand ways, the rules of healthy development.

  – Elizabeth Blackwell

Do not allow tobacco to dominate you.

- Pay no attention to what the critics say. Remember, a statue has never been erected in honour of a critic.

  – Jean Sibelius

- People are always asking about the good old days. I say, why don't you say the good now days.

  – Robert M Young

- People demand freedom of speech to make up for the freedom of thought which they avoid.

  – Soren Aabye Kierkegaard

- People do not always say what they mean or mean what they say.

  – James Patterson

- People do not make wars; governments do.

  – Ronald Reagan

- Politics is not a game. It is an earnest business.

  – Winston Churchill

- Prohibition is better than no liquor at all.

  – Will Rogers

- Protest beyond the law is not a departure from democracy, it is absolutely essential to it.

  – Howard Zinn

- Quality is everyone's responsibility.

  – W. Edwards Deming

- Q. What do you want to remember you as, The President of our country or a Scientist? asked Namita, Mangalore.

  A. As a good human being (A.P.J. Abdul Kalam).

People buy tobacco from his wealth.
But it is dangerous for health.

- Repetition of a truth is a lie.

  – Jiddu Krishnamurthi

- Science is always wrong, it never solves a problem without creating ten more.

  – George Bernard Shaw

- Shoot for the moon. Even you miss, you will land among the stars.

  – Les Brown

- Show me a thoroughly satisfied man and I will show you a failure.

  – Thomas A Edison

- Silence is not always golden. Sometimes it is guilt.

  – Annon

- Small acts, when multiplied by millions of people, can transform the world.

  – Howard Zinn

- Some are kissing mothers and some are scolding mothers, but it is love just the same.

  – Pearl Buck

- Some of us think, more of us think, we think, and most of us do not even think of thinking.

  – Herbert N. Casson

- Some people are so busy learning the tricks of the trade that they never learn the trade.

  – Vernon Law

- Some people will never learn anything because they understand everything too soon.

  – Alexander Pope

Cigarette: Make your choice.
It is your life – love it or burn it.

- Some rise by sin, and some by virtue fall.

  – William Shakespeare

- "Sometimes, we a nation of billion people, think like a nation of million people."

  – A.P.J. Abdul Kalam

- Something which we think is impossible now is not impossible in another decade.

  – Constance Baker Motley

- Sooner or later we all quote our mothers.

  – Bern Williams

- Speak softly and carry a big stick, you will go far.

  – Theodore Roosevelt

- Start by doing what is necessary, then do what is possible, and suddenly you are doing the impossible.

  – Saint Francis of Assisi

- Stop worrying about the potholes in the road and celebrate the journey!

  – Barbara Hoffman

- Success will not lower its standard to us. We must raise our standard to success.

  – Rev. Randall R. McBride jr

- Suicide is a permanent solution to a temporary problem.

  – Phil Donahue

- Taste can not be controlled by law.

  – Thomas Jefferson

- Tears may be dried up, but the heart never.

  – Marguerite de Valois

Smokers also have decreased vision at night.

- Tears always do not tell us the truth.

– P. Brunton

- Technology will change, products can come and go but brands can live forever.

– N. Prem Anand

- The beginning is the most important part of the work.

– Plato

- The biggest problem in the world could have been solved when it was small.

– Witter Bynner

- The cat having sat upon a hot stove lid, will not sit upon a hot stove lid again. But she would not sit upon a cold stove lid, either.

– Mark Twain

- The cost of living is going up and the chance of living is going down.

– Flip Wilson

- The crowd gives the leader new strength.

– Evenius

- The day you were born, a ladder was set up to help you escape from this world.

– Sufi Saying

- The difference between a helping hand and an outstretched palm is a twist of the wrist.

– Laurence Leamer

- The difference between ordinary and extraordinary is that little extra.

– Jimmy Johnson

Cancer may have started the fight but I will finish it.

- The distance is nothing, it is only the first step that is difficult.

  – Marie De Vichy-Chaconne

- The easiest way to be cheated is to believe yourself to be more cunning than others.

  – Pierr Charron

- The employer generally gets the employees he deserves.

  – J. Paul Getty

- The first half of our lives is ruined by our parents, and the second half by our children.

  – Clarence Darrow

- The future is today.

  – William Osler

- The greatest risk is the risk of riskless living.

  – Stephen R Covey

- The heart knows nothing of the past, nothing of the future, it knows only of the present. The heart has no time concept.

  – Osho Quotes

- The illiterate of the 21st century will not be those who can not read and write, but those who cannot learn, unlearn, relearn.

  – Alvin Toffler

- The internet is the Viagra of big business.

  – Jack Welch

- The key to finding beauty is to know where to look.

  – Siegfried and Roy

- The lie is a condition of life.

  – Friedrich Nietzsche

It is never too late to give up smoking.

- The living moment is everything.

  – D.H. Lawrence

- The mind is not a vessel to be filled but a fire to be kindled.

  – Plutarch

- The more alternatives, the more difficult the choice.

  – Abbe 'D' Allanival

- The more you praise and celebrate your life, the more there is in life to celebrate.

  – Oprah Winfrey

- The most important thing is not which system do you use – the most important thing is that you have a system.

  – PWCS, Management Consultant

- The most interesting thing about a postage stamp is the persistence with which it sticks to its job.

  – Napoleon Hill

- The only reward for love is the experience of loving.

  – John le Carre

- The past does NOT equal the future.

  – Anthony Robbins

- The poor, the unsuccessful, the unhappy, the unhealthy are the ones who use the word tomorrow the most.

  – Robert Kiyosaki

- The reason why worry kills more people than work is that more people worry than work.

  – Robert Frost

Choose life not tobacco.

- The remedy is worse than the disease.

  – Francis Bacon

- The reward of a thing well done is having done it.

  – Ralph Waldo Emerson

- The rule is, jam tomorrow and jam yesterday – but never jam today.

  – Lewis Carroll

- The secret of your future is hidden in your daily routine. Your future results from daily effort.

  – Mike Murdock

- The shoe that fits one person pinches another, there is no recipe for living that suits all cases.

  – Carl Jung

- The trouble with weather forecasting is that it's right too often for us to ignore it and wrong too often for us to rely on it.

  – Patrick Young

- The true meaning of life is to plant trees, under whose shade you do not expect to sit.

  – Nelson Henderson

- The will to win is important, but the will to prepare is vital.

  – Joe Paterno

- The world is round, it has no points.

  – Adrienne E. Gusoff

- The worst men often give the best advice.

  – Francis Bacon

- The young man knows the rules, but the old man knows the exceptions.

  – Oliver Wendell Holmes

Yoga significantly helps to fight breast cancer.

- There are two kinds of people, those who do the work and those who take the credit. Try to be in the first group, where there is less competition.

  – Indira Gandhi

- Theirs is not to make reply. Theirs is not to reason why. Theirs is but to do and die.

  – Alfred Lord Tennyson

- There are no facts, only interpretations.

  – Friedrich Nietzsche

- There are no speed limit on the road to excellence.

  – David W Johnson

- There are two ways of exerting one's strength: one is pushing down, the other is pulling up.

  – Booker T. Washington

- There is no pleasures in a fight but some of my fights have been a pleasure to win.

  – Muhammad Ali

- There is no present. There is only the immediate future and the recent past.

  – George Carlin

- There is no such thing as public opinion. There is only published opinion.

  – Winston Churchill

- There is nothing politically right that is morally wrong.

  – Daniel O'Connell

- There is nothing stronger in the world than gentleness.

  – Han Suyin

Patients own vigilance & clinician's alertness are the primary ways in detecting early onset of cancer.

- There may be luck in getting a good job – but there's no luck in keeping it.

  – J. Ogden Armour

- There was a very cautious man who never laughed or cried. He never risked, he never lost, he never won nor tried. And when he one day passed away his insurance was denied, for since he never really lived, they claimed he never died.

  – Empires of the Mind

- Things do not happen. Things are made to happen.

  – John F. Kennedy

- This is a court of law, young man, not a court of justice.

  – Oliver Wendell Holmes

- Till I was 13, I thought my name was "Shut Up".

  – Joe Namath

- Time is the most valuable thing a man can spend.

  – Theophrastus

- To avoid criticism, do nothing, say nothing, and be nothing.

  – Elbert Hubbard

- To do nothing is sometimes a good remedy.

  – Hippocrates

- To forget good is not good, immediately to forget what is not good is good.

  – Thiruvalluvar

Tambakoo hai aisa zahar
zo barbaad kar deta hai ghar.

- Too light winning makes the prize light.

– William Shakespeare

- True friends stab you in the front.

– Oscar wilde

- Trust, but verify.

– Ronald Reagan

- Try not to be a man of success rather be a man of value.

– Albert Einstein

- Try to learn something about everything and everything about something.

– Thomas H. Huxley

- TV is chewing gum for the eyes.

– Frank Lloyd Wright

- Vision is the art of seeing things invisible.

– Jonathan Swift

- Vote for the man who promises least, he will be the least disappointing.

– Bernard Baruch

- War does not determine who is right – only who is left.

– Bertrand Russell

- Washington is the only place where sound travels faster than light.

– C.V.R. Thompson

- We all have to take defeats in life.

– Muhammad Ali

Cancer survivors turned global cancer ambassadors with mission at U.N.

- We are never deceived; we deceive ourselves.

– Johann Wolfgang Von Goethe

- We are not human beings having a spiritual experience. We are spiritual beings having a human experience.

-Pierre Teihard de Chardin

- We are taught to fly in the air like birds, and to swim in the water like fishes, but how to live on the earth we do not know.

– Dr. S. Radhakrishnan

- We can't help everyone, but everyone can help someone.

– Ronald Reagan

- We do not succeed in changing things according to our desire, but gradually our desire changes.

– Marcel Proust

- We hate some persons because we do not know them; and we will not know them because we hate them.

– Charles Caleb Colton

- We have to hate our immediate predecessors to get free of their authority.

– D.H. Lawrence

- We make a living by what we get, but we make a life by what we give.

– Winston Churchill

- We make war so that we may live in peace.

– Aristotle

- Weather forecast for tonight, dark, continued dark overnight.

Jo hai tumhen tambakoo se pyaar,
cancer ka milega tumhe upahar.

– George Carlin

- What we do to impress others are the very things others find most annoying.

  – Burke Franklin

- What we obtain too cheap, we esteem too lightly, it is dearness only that gives everything its value.

  – Burke Franklin

- What we see depends mainly on what we look for.

  – John Lubbock

- What you resist, persists and grows larger.

  – Jeanne Bice

- When a man wants to murder a tiger, he calls it sport, when a tiger wants to murder him, he calls it ferocity.

  – George Bernard shaw

- When God solves your problems you have faith in His abilities, when God does not solve your problems, He has faith in your abilities.

  – Rishika (Posted on May 16,2011)

- When I read about the evils of drinking, I gave up reading.

  – Henny Youngman

- When I was born, I was so surprised. I did not talk for a year and a half.

  – Gracie Allen

- When the candles are out, all women are fair.

  – Plutarch

- When the sea was calm, all ships alike showed mastership in floating.

  – William Shakespeare

Cancer ko jo hai dur bhagaana, tambakoo, zarda, kabhi na khana.

- When we see a big white clothes with a black dot, what do we see? We look at problems in opportunities instead of looking at opportunities in problems.

  – Jalaludin Rumi

- When we're unhappy, God smiles at us. When we're happy, God laughs at us. But when we make other happy, God salutes us.

  – Charlie Chaplin

- When written in Chinese, the word "CRISIS" is composed of two characters. One represents danger and the other represents opportunity.

  – John F. Kennedy

- When you judge another, you do not define them, you define yourself.

  – Wayne Dyer

- When you say you agree to a thing in principle, you mean that you have not the slightest intention of carrying it out in practice.

  – Otto Von Bismarck

- When you want to fool the world, tell the truth.

  – Otto Von Bismarck

- Whenever there is a hard job to be done, I assign it to a lazy man, he is sure to find an easy way of doing it.

  – Walter Chrysler

- Where annual elections end where slavery begins.

  – John Quincy Adams

Public places and transport: Better be tobacco free.

- Where facts are few, experts are many.

  – Donald R Gannon

- Wherever you go, go with all your heart.

  – Confucius

- Winners make it happen. Losers let it happen.

  – Leonard Lavin

- Winners never quit and quitters never win.

  – Vince Lombardi

- Winning is a habit. Unfortunately, so is losing.

  – Vince Lombardi

- With love and patience, nothing is impossible.

  – Daisaku Ideda

- Without deviation from the norm, progress is not possible.

  – Frank Zappa

- Yesterday is beyond repair; tomorrow may never come; today alone is ours; make the best use of it as; it is your sole, sure possession.

  – Zarathustra

- Yesterday is history, tomorrow is a mystery, and today is a gift – that is why we call it "The Present".

  – Brian G Dyson

- You call it madness, but I call it love.

  – Don Byas

- You can't trust water – Even a straight stick turns crooked in it.

  – W.C. Fields

Make tobacco free film, tobacco free fashion.

- You change your life by changing your heart.

  – Max Lucado

- You don't take a photograph, you make it.

  – Ansel Adams

- You never conquer a mountain. Mountains cannot be conquered. You only conquer yourself.

  – Jim Whitaker

- You will do foolish things, but do them with enthusiasm.

  – Colette

- Your attitude, not your aptitude, will determine your altitude.

  – Zig Ziglar

- Your best teacher is your last mistake.

  – Ralph Nader

- Your children need your presence more than your presents.

  – Jesse Jackson

- Your future depends on many things, but mostly on you.

  – Frank Tyger

- Youth has no age.

  – Pablo Picasso

- Zen Quotes : When the pupil is ready to learn, a teacher will appear.

  – Lao Tzu

Quitting smoking is hard,
but consequence of not quitting is harder.

Enjoy Axiom

THE HIGH QUOTE

30 Per cent of the cases filed by the government officials were basically clamours for "higher wages, more holidays and desire to do no work". The Delhi High Court thinks something like this:

"Prabhu chakri aisi dijiye,
Kaam kachu na hoye,
Mooh manga vetan mile,
Hardin chutti hoye."

(Lord, give me a job which requires no work to be done. Make sure the wages are as I wish and everyday is a holiday.

– The Indian Express, New Delhi, August 6, 2010

- Sound sleep is a fundamental right of a citizen.
  – Delhi High Court: H.T., Patna, March 30, 2011

- A poor man sleeps sound.

- It is better to be first citizen than second citizen abroad.

Adage: *Ideal thoughts tutored to us in childhood (German motto):*

If money is lost, nothing is lost,
If health is lost, something is lost,
If character is lost everything is lost.

The first health is wealth.
Happy health, happy life.

Global Version in 21st Century:

If character is lost, nothing is lost,
If health is lost, something is lost,
If money is lost, everything is lost.

- A "Character Certificate" from foreign journals seems to excite our politicians.
- A black man being called Mr. White.
- A closed mind is seldom opened easily.
- A disciplinarian is one who can make students laugh heartily in a disciplined way.
- A dog is the only animal on this earth that loves you more than himself.
- A gold is tested in four ways by rubbing, cutting, beating and polishing.
- A good deed brings its own rewards to young soul.
- A good lawyer is a bad neighbour.
- A good man dies when a boy goes wrong.
- A huge tree gives shade during the day, becomes the shelter for birds at night.
- A leader's glory is magnified by his followers.
- A lot of trouble is caused in this world by combining a narrow mind with a wide mouth.
- A Loyal cum Royal employee faces the brunt of his colleagues after Boss is transferred.

Early discovery, early recovery.

- A man is known by the company he avoids. Better be alone than in a bad company.
- A man's best friend are his TEN fingers.
- A miser has ever ready refusals.
- A pill in time saves nine.
- A private life of a public personality is the talk of the town.
- A retired officer – I am completely out of the Rules and Regulations of my Organisation.
- A road sign :

  Left is always right.
- A serpent dies if it climbs upon a palm tree.
- A sign board on a Photostat Shop: Photostat is done in all languages.
- A smile is an expression not a feeling.
- A successful man is one who makes more money so that his wife can spend. A successful woman is one who can find such a man.
- A Sunday well-spent brings a week of content.
- A thing when lost is valued most.
- A tree laden with fruits attracts more stones.
- A variety of colours make up the beauty and that's why the rainbow is beautiful.

Cancer is preventable, cancer is treatable.

- A word of encouragement during a failure is worth more than an hour of praise after success.
- A Yogi must avoid the two extremes of luxury and austerity.
- ABBREVIATION: Why is abbreviation such a long word ?
- Action may not always bring happiness, but there is no happiness without action.
- Admitting you are wrong is a modest way of showing you have grown a little wiser.
- After the heated exchange, between the ledger keeper and Accountant, the ledger keeper wrote "Accountant Closed" instead of account closed deliberately.
- After your hands become coated with grease, your nose will begin to itch.
- Agriculture – Agree to your Boss is the culture of an organisation nowadays.
- All are not thieves that dogs bark at.
- All roads lead to "No smoking".
- Always say less than necessary as humans are machines of interpretation and explanation.
- Amazing wealth often ruins health.
- An excuse is worse and more terrible than a lie, for an excuse is a lie guarded.

Everyone should be his own physician.

- An interesting question is how simple is simple? Our poet Ghalib sang: "How difficult it is to make anything simple. Even man finds it hard to be human".
- An objection is not a rejection, it is simply a request for information.
- An ounce of prevention is worth a pound of cure. Hospitals merely replace "Physical pain" with "Financial drain".
- Anger is a condition when the tongue works faster than mind.
- Answer in brief.
- Anyone can be polite to a king, but it takes a civilised person to be polite to a beggar.
- Anywhere is paradise, it is upto you.
- Arrogant people cannot get guidance.
- Ask me no questions, I'll tell you no lies.
- Ask! Ask! Ask! Why people are afraid to ask?
- Assets and Liabilities – Brain as assets and stomach as liabilities.
- At the age of twenty, we do not care what the world thinks of us. At thirty, we worry about what it is thinking about us. At forty, we discover that it was not thinking of us.
- Attachment is a source of pain.

Do not make your lungs ashtray.

- Avail the opportunity, before the opportunity expires.
- Average is the poorest of the good and the best of the bad.
- Avoid eating even vegetarian food in Non-Vegetarian Hotels.
- Bad habits are easier to abandon today than tomorrow.
- Bank Officer, Private Clinic, First Delivery always attracts caesarean.
- Be child but not childish.
- Be gentle with the earth.
- Be good yourself without expecting people to call you good. "What a big blunder is to expect that people call you good!" Give up the desire to be called good but be good.
- Be not afraid of growing slowly, be afraid of standing still.
- Beauty weeps while fortune enjoys.
- Bees that have honey in the mouths have stings in their tails.
- Behind every successful man there are a lot of unsuccessful years.
- Behind every successful man there is a woman, and behind every unsuccessful man there is also a woman.

Cancer cures smoking.

- Better half or bitter half.
- "Bharat Sarkar" or "Ashoka Stambha" sign – A road to passport.
- Bhaskaracharya proved that zero divided by zero was neither zero nor one, but infinity.
- "*Bhoot Pisach nikat nahin aave Mahabeer Jab naam sunave.*"

  It is the most popular verse (Chaupai) of Shri Hanuman Chalisa, especially amongst children, written by Tulsidas.
- Borrowed garments never fit well.
- Building trust takes time.
- Business has no limit.
- Can you imagine a shirt without a button. Although a button is very small it has a special place in your life.
- Carelessness is injurious.
- Caution : Do not open your mouth until brain is in gear.
- Change is not made without inconvenience, even from worse to better.
- Change of home town change the status. Our capabilities are in the area in which we are good. The crocodile is strong in water and toy for children in the sand.

Smoking – Quit it before your life quits you.

- Charity always feels better to the donor than to the recipient.
- Charity begins at home but should not end there.
- Charity sees the need not the cause.
- Choose “what is right” and “who is right”.
- Chunnu Munnu (CM) is not only the popular name of a child during fifties and sixties but the light work/easy problem is also called CM.
- Circle has no directions. Life is a full circle – *Khabhi Khushi Khabhi Gam.*
- Clever man must introspects himself first.
- Colours influence us a lot.
- Colours speak all languages.
- “Common Cold” is the most common disease that spreads by contact.
- Common sense – Crown of all facilities. Why do we call ‘common’ sense if it is so uncommon?
- Consider your office, whatever its size, as your home.
- Corruption begins at home. The people’s mindset is prone to corruption.
- Couples hold hands during their wedding because it is a formality just like two boxers sharing hands before the fight begins!

Columbus discovered tobacco.

- Dare to be wise.
- Dare to fail and fall.
- Dealing with corrupt officer is easy and convenient than honest man in business.
- Delay is not always a problem, sometimes it is a solution.
- Department of Forest – Department for rest. Gantantra – GUN Tantra.
- Detecting is not proving.
- Discovery is a process without a recess.
- Do important jobs before they become urgent.
- Do not carry atlas on your head.
- Do not employ handsome servant. Handsome servant means hands up husband.
- Do not look where you fell, but where you slipped.
- Do not open a shop unless you like to smile.
- Do not ride if you can walk.
- Do not run away from death, you can never die before the appointed time and nothing can save you from dying when the appointed time comes.
- Dogs do not dislike poor families.
- Dowry – A bridegroom is turned into a bribedgroom.

Choose life not tabacco.

- Dying men speak true.
- Earlier, we opposed computerisation as it retrenched staff (1:10). But today computerisation (I.T) has provided highest number of jobs.
- East or West, Home is the Best.
- Eat slowly.
- Efficiency increases in crisis. Leaders are also born out of crisis (situation).
- Etc. is a symbol used to make others believe we know more than what we do.
- Even a stopped clock is right twice a day.
- Even mosquito does not get a pat on the back until the mosquito acts well.
- Even the lion has to defend himself against flies.
- Even you do thankless job, you may get thanks. Thanks is losing its shine due to frequent use. Express gratitude.
- Every creature loves first then enjoys sex.
- Every generalisation can be dangerous.
- Every law has loops and holes.
- Every mission must have a vision.
- Every particle of a holy thing is also holy. (*Narmada ke Kankkar sabhi Shivshankar.*)

Be a non-smoker.

- Every prize has its price. The prize is yes, the price is no.
- Every sun set gives us one day less to live, but every sun rise gives us one more day to hope. So, hope for the best.
- Every surprise is not a prize.
- Every WORD is a mantra.
- Everybody cries in "Mother tongue". Nobody cries in "Foreign language". Everybody sees dreams in "Mother tongue".
- Everybody feels and expresses, however, the power of expression is not the same in all.
- Everybody is wise after the event.
- Everybody's business is nobody's business.
- Everyone has his own story to tell.
- Everyone is entitled to be stupid, but some abuse the privilege.
- Everyone wants to command, and no one wants to obey.
- Everything happens in due course.
- Everything is funny as long as it is happening to someone else.
- Everything is God and God's everything. So, God is one.
- Exception proves the rule. Children are not served betel (Paan).

Avoid passive smoking. It is too dangerous.

- Exercise is insurance.
- Extend courtesy to others not because they are gentlemen but because you are gentleman.
- Fall seven times, stand up eight.
- False target makes the employee liar.
- Fast ripe, fast rotten.
- Fasting and feasting cannot be everlasting.
- Fasting is of value today, has always been in the past and will be in the future too.
- Feed someone well and you will get blessing in return.
- FIFO – First In First Out (ATM: Transaction)

  LIFO – Last In First Out (Teeth: Hard and Strong)

  FILO – First In Last Out (Tongue: Soft and Gentle)
- Fight procrastination.
- Fingerprint of a person remains unchanged throughout his life.
- Fire does not burn 'thoroughly burnt objective'.
- First April, not always is a day of fools. Reserve Bank of India started functioning from 1st April, 1935.
- First they ignore you, then they laugh at you, then fight with you and then you win.

Leave tabacco, live happily.

- For enhancing your value – *Kaam kum karo. Kaam ki fikr karo aur fikr ka zikr karo.*
- Freedom is freedom. Be free like the clouds.
- Full stomach makes a jolly-heart.
- Gandhiji always travelled in 3rd class because there was no 4th class.
- Garden – A thing of beauty, is a job forever.
- General 'M' – All the people in the age group between 35 to 45 years of age, M stands for Middle. Out of 26 alphabets, the central alphabets that is number 13 is M.
- Generation to generation, we live in "Age of Ignorance".
- Geographic boundaries to knowledge have been erased.
- Give to the world the best you have, the best will come back to you.
- Giving and receiving gifts – A norm in business if appropriate. If not appropriate – either "Thoughtless" or a "Bribe".
- Go on meeting people (cold visits).
- God does not ask about our ability, but our availability.
- God is with us on all the ways and always. But are we with Him?
- Going downward is very easy.

Taste tobacco, taste death.

- Good teachers cover up for infrastructure handicaps. They build generations.
- Good, better, best never rest, till good is better and better be the best.
- Gradual progress – the raw sugar cane is first crushed and the juice is extracted from there. The liquid juice is then boiled, and made into solid sugar, which is then refined and turned into fine crystallised sugar. So, in order to obtain particular result in certain cases, you have to assume a severe, stern and unyielding attitude.
- Growing only in age for what?
- Gulab Jamun neither posses Gulab nor Jamun, still it is known as Gulab Jamun.
- Half the people lie with their lips; the other half with their tears.
- *Hamare Desh Mein Khel Ek Samasya Hai aur Samasya Ek Khel Hai.*
- Handwriting is not really just the hand writing. It is more of mind writing.
- Happiness and not sorrow is the end and aim of everyone.
- Happy Child Nation's Pride.
- Hard work never killed anybody.
- Hatred is much harder to fake love. You hear of fake love; never of fake hate.

Love tobacco, love death.

- Having one child makes you a parent, having two, a referee.
- He who conquers himself is greater than the commander-in-chief, who conquers a country.
- He who fails to prepare, prepares to fail.
- He who laughs last, thinks slowest.
- He would milk you whether you have teats or not.
- Health is not valued till sickness comes.
- Heart makes nature (*Swabhav*) and mind makes behaviour (*Vyawahar*).
- Help ever, hurt never.
- High jump needs long run.
- Home is where the heart is.
- Honesty does not succeed in dealing with a villain.
- Honesty is still the Best Policy.
- "Hum Aapke Hai Kaun": the Hindi Film – a super hit was released in Europe as "yours forever".
- Husband and wife are one in two or two in one.
- Hygiene is two-third of health.
- I am retired – good bye tension, hello pension.
- I am safaring (travelling) after retirement.

Each one teach one, tobacco – "House of Hell".

- I clear your vision: says Spectacles.
- I like you, you love me, he loves me. It is not a tense but suspense.
- I want to marry a girl not that I can live with her but I cannot live without her.
- I will start tomorrow. Tomorrow is a disease.
- Idea rules the world.
- Ideally, governments should collect taxes like a honeybee, which sucks just the right amount of honey from the flower so that both can survive.
- If a dust is placed in a dustbin then it is not called dust.
- If a new city is created, many creatures are uprooted.
- If any one feels, he is indispensable makes him dispensable at any cost.
- If any thing has a beginning, it must have an end, and if it has a beginning and an end, it has a middle also.
- If everybody would have similar thoughts, then the doors to progress would be shut.
- If in doubt, leave it out.
- If it is not right, don't do it.
- If one is not afraid of anything, make him afraid of "Dharma".

Cancer patients struggle with expenses.
Attendants feel tired.

- If people are counting the number of okays in your speech, it is not okay. They are not hearing what you are saying.
- If the priority of something goes up, the priority of something else comes down.

  Example : Pulse Polio sidelined many other medical drives. Cricket shadowed almost all games in India .
- If there is a rumour, there is definitely someone planting it.
- If there were more than one God, the heaven and earth would have been in a state of disorder.
- If you are alert, dreams will not take place.
- If you argue with a woman and win, you lose.
- If you change queues, the one you have left will start to make faster than the one you are in now.
- If you do not want long discussion by the Cabinet on specific agenda put it as the last agenda before lunch.
- If you lend a friend Rs. 1000, you lose either a friend or Rs.1000.
- If you lie to me, keep lying, don't hurt me by suddenly telling the truth.
- If you make others laugh, it is equivalent to doing social service.

Tobacco is a knife that cuts your life.

- If you see no reason for giving thanks, the fault lies in yourself.
- If you want others to be happy, practice compassion. If you want to be happy, practice compassion.
- If you want people to read a book, tell them it is overrated.
- If you want to annoy a poet, explain his poetry.
- If you will do good, people will accuse you of selfish ulterior motives – Do good anyway.
- If you will not NIP in the bud, all wrongful will become rightful. If anyone will urinate or spit paan at any corner/place, with the passage of time, it will be a certified centre.
- If your batting average is high enough, the big league will find you.
- If your problem has a solution then why worry about it. If your problem does not have a solution, why worry about it.
- Ignorance of law is no excuse.
- Improve water quality and increase water quantity for community.
- In a Hotel: "We provide only home not rooms."
- In a mango groove, there may be some other trees, but still people call it a mango groove.
- In all festivals, we all cherish our childhood celebration of festivals and share it all the times.

Cancer is there, where there is tobacco, so beware.

- In almost all the languages of the world, the word for "Mother" begins with M-Sound.
- In Bank, if you are not found suitable (say *Nikamma*) by your Boss, he will even then request for your suitable replacement before relieving you on transfer.
- In great attempts, it is glorious to fail.
- In journalism, a bikini headline is one that covers the main point of the story.
- In life you are either a passenger or a pilot, it is your choice.
- In most sports, you are reacting to someone else, but in GOLF (Game of Life First) you are reacting to your own performance. No Blame Game in Golf.
- In order to become the master, the politician poses as the servant.
- In performance review meeting only non-performance is reviewed.
- In politics, there is no friend or foe.
- In Tennis, Table Tennis, Badminton, "Love" means "Zero"(Love All/Five Love).
- In the ant's house, the dew is a flood.
- In WAR there is no second prize for the runner-up.
- In Webster's Unabridged dictionary, 66 column inches are devoted for the definition of the word

Many a time I have found myself smoking without being aware of it.

"Take" but only 22 column inches for the world "Give". So more takers and few givers.

- In yesteryears when the Head Peon used to come out of Boss Office, every one was afraid to hear – "*Sahib Ne Yaad Kiya Hai*".
- Income tax: 150 years of Building India.
- Indeed, it is quite interesting to observe that when father helps his son to walk, both laugh; when a son helps his father to walk, both cry.
- India is the only country where Lakshmi is worshipped.
- India needs more "Lavatory" than "Laboratory".
- Inflation is being broke with a lot of money in your pocket.
- Information is power.
- Inquire within.
- Intelligence – Knowing when to stay dumb especially in front of one's boss.
- Interest of the world is the interest of one's own.
- It is a funny thing about life. If you refuse to accept anything but the best you very often get it.
- It is better to fight for something than against something.
- It is easier to cheat a dishonest person.

When I do not have cigarettes with me, I get panicky and even sweat.

- It is not beneficial to be simple or to be upright. It is self destructive. Go to the forest and see for yourself that straight trees are cut down early and easily, while the crooked and hunch backed stand untouched.
- It is not only your image, but it is your imagination which makes a difference.
- It is not that people are useless, the unfortunate part is that they are USED-less.
- It is the last inch that counts. A miss by an inch is a miss by a mile.
- It is the women who shop but the men who carry the bags home?
- *Jo Hua So Hua* – It is not a Chinese language but widely spoken in North India.
- Joys are multiplied and sorrows are divided by sharing.
- Judge – Sit on the Bench after a long Standing at the Bar.
- Jumping to conclusions can be a bad exercise.
- Justice delayed is justice denied. Justice hurried is justice buried.
- *Katcha Chittha* is *Pucca Chittha* in bussiness and *Pucca Chittha* is *Katcha Chittha* likewise.

Smoking is not a "Pipe of Peace".

- Keep your mind on the things you want and off the things you do not want.
- King has many ears and eyes.
- "Knowingly people do not have time to help others, but unknowingly they always have time to hurt others."
- KYC- Not only "Know Your Customer" but also "Know Your Competitor".
- Ladies and Gentlemen, the Guest of Honour this evening needs no introduction as he did not turn up!
- Ladies first, pretty ladies sooner.
- Laughter is the best medicine. But in Helena, America, this medicine was banned after 7 p.m. No one was allowed to laugh after 7 p.m.
- Laziness travels so slowly that poverty soon overtakes him.
- Learn the "Art of Stress Free Life" and also try to learn the "Art of Shifting Stress upstairs to lead Stress Free Life".
- Learn the rules so you know how to break them properly.
- Learning and breathing are life long phenomenon.
- Life is not without pain and doubt.
- Life is to live, let live and forgive.

If you smoke, then all the hazards of smoking apply to you.

- Light is the life of lamp.
- Lightning never strikes twice at the same place.
- Like your staff, hike your business.
- Literacy is a great leveller.
- Live life king-size.
- Lok Sabha Speaker seldom speaks.
- Longer life does not guarantee healthier life.
- Look at your eyes, they are so small but they can see enormous things.
- Love at first sight, but it is always better to have a second look.
- Love is blind but marriage is the eye opener.
- Luck is always against the one who depends on it.
- Luck sometimes visits a fool, but never sits down with him.
- Man dies, but his name survives.
- Man has one thing at heart, and expresses quite a different thing by words.
- Manner first, matter later.
- Many people are vegetarian by birth but few by conviction.
- Marriage is a relationship in which one person is right and other is husband.

Life is a cigarette which begins with flashes but ends in the ashes.

- Marriage is like a pack of cards. When courting, it is hearts. When you are engaged, it is diamonds. After marriage, it is clubs. And at the end, it is spades.

- Marriages are made in heaven. But internet is where nagging spouses are put on sale.

- Matrimony – MATTER-O-MONEY.

- Make hay while your luck shines.

- Medicines though cure disease but can not rule out that they have no side effects.

- Memory gives both pain and pleasure.

- Money has no ears but it hears.

- Money talks. But not to everyone.

- More haste, less speed.

- More important than cost of living is at whose cost we are living.

- Most of our time is spent in solving problems created by ourselves and others.

- Mother's Day – Nine months after "Father's Night".

- My Credit Card expired, burial today, revival tomorrow.

- My creditor died last night, so I am looking bright and happy.

To help and educate people quit smoking.

- Nature has given two ears and one mouth.
- Nature's offence, no defence.
- Never mind whom you promise, but be very careful whom you blame.
- Never say 'no' twice, if you mean it.
- New Lords, New Laws.
- NGO receives 'Aid' to protect 'Aids'.
- Nipper is the name of the dog in HMV'S (Gramophone) Logo (Emblem).
- No answer is also an answer.
- No author should be considered as having failed until he starts teaching others about writing.
- No company can exist without customer.
- No creature other than human can laugh.
- No do or die but do it and die.
- No man is wise at all times.
- No one can love whole night.
- No one loves the man whom he fears.
- No process of the body takes place in isolation.
- No road is long with good company.
- Nobody can do everything but everyone can do something.

Leave tobacco and say all is well.

- Nobody likes complaints but everybody complains.
- Not approved deliberately altered as note approved.
- Nothing in excess.
- Nothing is more permanent than "temporary" arrangements, and nothing is more temporary than "permanent" ones.
- Nothing is to last forever. Everyone, everything is gone, is going, and will go.
- Nothing seems expensive on credit.
- Nourish your work and flourish in your job.
- Nowadays people know the price of everything and the value of nothing.
- Office without pay makes thieves.
- Officers, generally, clamour for more financial power but when they get increased power, they seldom use it.
- Okay (Ok.) is the world's most recognised word.
- Old age is second childhood.
- OLYMPICS – International sporting event in which we lose at almost everything except BLAME GAME.
- On birthdays and other auspicious occasions, people in India light wick lamps. In western countries on such occasions, lighted candles are put out.

Life is precious, keep away tobacco.

- On the examination of teeth, true nature of a man can be ascertained.
- One day is lost if we have not laughed even once.
- One diabetic is quarreling with another diabetic to take a sweet revenge.
- One feels proud to be Non-Resident Indian as government provides every possible facilities to him than to Indians.
- One half of the world does not know how the other half lives.
- One is never at ease in other's house.
- One of the most common cause of failure is the habit of quitting.
- One thing is certain nowadays i.e., every thing is uncertain.
- One who reigns over the heart of everyone is a king.
- One woman never praises another.
- Onion tears do not touch the heart.
- Only a crowd can make you feel so alone.
- Opportunity comes but does not linger.
- Our body is alkaline by design and acid-producing by function.
- Our pleasures are always changing.

Adopt healthy life line. Give up tobacco line.

- Our scientific power has outrun our spiritual power. We have guided missiles and misguided men.
- Out of debt, out of danger.
- Out sourcing – Now "sleep" is also out sourced by taking "sleeping pills".
- Over eating invites disease.
- Patience is a virtue.
- People appreciate but do not encourage.
- People are fearless because of fear in most of the countries. A fearful man always suffer from fears.
- People fear from the cyclone. Do cyclones not rise in people's mind.
- People used to wear ordinary clothes weekdays and formal attire on Sunday. Today, it is exactly the reverse.
- People usually apologise so that they can do it again.
- Permanent prosperity is impossible without noble deeds.
- Plan your day the night before.
- Planning "*Hosh Se Karo*" aur implement "*Josh Se Karo*".

When you smoke a cigarette your throat is like a factory chimney, a bus exhaust pipe, or a garden bonfire.

- Politicians must be allowed to panic. They need activity. It is their substitute for achievement.
- 'Positive' anything is better than 'negative' nothing.
- Praise makes good men better and bad men worse.
- Pray as if everything depends on God. And work as if everything depends upon you.
- Preach the need for change, but never reform too much at once.
- Press the nose, and the mouth will open.
- Prices – The only thing which violates the law of gravity.
- Problem solving is a life time's work, you're engaged in it all the time.
- Prosperity gathers friend.
- Put values first, everything else will follow into place.
- Quite revealing of human preferences that more suicides come from shame or loss of financial and social status than medical diagnosis.
- Regrets and fear are twin thieves that rob us of today, regret of yesterday and fear of tomorrow.
- Remain undisturbed in disturbing situation to arrive at a solution to the problem.
- Remember Rajiv Gandhi's immortal words: "*Hum Jeetengey ya losengey*".

Ta ta to tobacco, bye bye to cancer.

- Retired but sex not expired.
- Retirement does not come as a surprise.
- Right is might.
- Rules are relaxed when times go hard.
- Rumours are only valuable when they are denied.
- Rural Market is now Global Market.
- Rush hour– When traffic is at a standstill.
- Science has not prevented rising incidence of disease.
- Seeing and feeling are quite 360°.
- Seeing is an art. Everybody does not know how to see.
- Seeing yourself bankrupt in dream forecast your prosperity.
- Selfless love is only the mother's love.
- Sell any cake like a hotcake.
- Sell like a great man. Give services like a mad man.
- She is not going beyond to a beauty parlour to make up her mind.
- Show love and care to a son until he is five years of age, and control him for the next ten years, but treat him as a friend when he attains his sixteenth year.

Eat tobacco, meet cancer.

- Six feet on earth makes all men equal, just do not measure it.
- Small is beautiful like L.L.B. But its full form is Legum Baccalaureus (Bachelor of Laws where LL is taken as "Laws").
- SMS is an indispensable part of life rather it is lifeline for the hearing impaired. "Deaf " used to talk through SMS with their counterpart.
- Some babies die by chance, none should die by choice.
- Some bans help, most make no sense. Like, cigarette smoking in public place, Please do not urinate here, Please do not pluck flowers, No parking, License for bicycle, rickshaw, bullock cart, tonga, etc.
- Someone decides the case on brief case to brief case basis and not case to case basis. (on Corruption)
- Some people's promises are like pie-crust, made to be broken.
- Somebody has said – "We stop playing because we are old. We grow old because we stop playing."
- Someone who says "I am busy" is either declaring incompetence (and lack of control of his life) or trying to get rid of you.
- Sometimes apologising does not mean that you are wrong and the other is right. It only means that you value the relationship much more than your ego.

Tobacco free nation, peoples pride.

Sometimes we thank nature. That is when nature is conducive we thank it and when not, we curse it but nature has its own rules.

- Spare the rod spare the child.
- Spend some time alone everyday.
- Spotted a board on the Delhi-Mathura road reading: If married, divorce speed. If you want to donate blood, do not do it on the road. Donate it in the blood bank. Donate Blood! It's a bloody good job.
- Stolen fruit is the sweetest.
- Stomach teaches all arts.
- STOP! Says the red light. Go! Says the green.
- Success comes only by keeping the planning secret.
- Success does not depend on making an important decision quickly. It only depends on your quick action against the important decision.
- Success is not the key to happiness. Happiness is the key to success.
- SUN Stroke or SON Stroke.
- Suspicion dies when you close your eyes.
- Switch off the light when it is bright.
- Take 3 steps forward, if needed go back 2 steps, you will be still one step forward, and go on. A lot of changes will take place.

Do not make mood with tobacco.

- Talk slowly but think quickly.
- Team work divides the task and multiplies the success.
- Tears are words, the heart cannot express.
- Tell enough, just enough – not too more, not too less.
- Tell me the truth and then run.
- Tell soft words, win hard hearts.
- The anger that benefits others is a good anger.
- The beautiful rainbow needs both the rain and the sunshine.
- The beauty and strength of the democracy is that it can uplift ordinary people to an extraordinary position.
- The beauty of a female acts upon the mind even of a sage.
- The best defence is a good offence.
- The best gifts are tied with heart strings.
- The best speakers are the best listeners. Learn to listen.
- The body does not need anything except "system". Give full attention to health.
- The calamity of the information age is that the toxicity of data increases much faster than its benefits.

Free from tobacco free from cancer.

- The cobbler always wears the worst shoes.
- The cocktail party – Use and abuse. Too much alcohol damages liver and career.
- The darkest hour is just before the dawn.
- The distance is nothing, it is only the first step that is the hardest.
- The fastest way to become rich is to socialise with the poor, the fastest way to become poor is to socialise with the rich.
- The future is either bright or black.
- The Great Wall of China is also shaken by the winds of global phenomena.
- The "good old days" are right now.
- The historian whose wife left him because he frequently raked up her past!
- The ladder of success is never crowded at the top. There is always room at the top.
- The light purse is a heavy curse.
- The man who does more than he is paid for, will soon be paid for more than he does.
- The milestone stands at its place. It does not reach the destination but direct the destination.
- The mob has many heads but no brains. Never follow the crowd.
- The model was stripped off her citizenship.

It is easier not to start smoking than to stop it later on.

- The moon is one but on agitated water it produces many reflections.
- The more we try to forget you, the more it disturbs our mind.
- The more you build Jails and Hospitals, it will soon be crowded.
- The more you say, the more likely you are to say something foolish and the more common appear, and less in control.
- The morning is wiser than evening.
- The most common of crimes is killing time.
- The most impressive example of tolerance is a Golden Wedding Anniversary.
- The most painful moments are not those we spend with uninteresting people, rather, they are those spent with uninteresting people trying hard to be interesting.
- The ocean of storms is situated on the moon. Amazingly it has no water.
- The oldest letter of alphabet is "O" unchanged in shape from early days.
- The only remedy for bad habits is counter habits. Change is inherent in every form.
- The only thing about saying that you're honest is that there will always be people to prove that you're not.

Careless disposal of cigarette ends with disaster, damage and severe environmental hazard.

- The only thing greater than the power of mind is the courage of the heart.
- The opposite of success isn't failure, it is name-dropping.
- The outcome of an Election may be decided by those who have not voted for.
- The pencil is mightier than the pen. The pen does not work in the zero gravity inside a space capsule.
- The person whose Receipts and Disbursements are equal is neither rich nor poor, and is, on the whole, quite happy.
- The reputation of a thousand years may be determined by the conduct of one hour.
- The rich gets richer. The poor gets children.
- The road to success is always under construction.
- The search for excellence is linked to self-respect.
- The stages of medical Treatment:

  ILL : FIRST STAGE

  PILL : SECOND STAGE

  BILL : THIRD STAGE

  WILL : FOURTH STAGE (sometimes)

The fact that when you light a cigarette it produces clouds of smoke rather than a burst of flame is highly significant.

- The strongest man in the world is he "who stands alone".
- The sun can be seen only in light of the sun.
- The sun evaporates water only to return it manifold in the form of rain.
- The tree is known by its fruits.
- The voice of the people is the voice of God.
- The way you think, the way you live.
- The will is almighty.
- The work praises the man.
- The worst thing about growing old is to listen a lot of advice from your children.
- There are many things in life that will catch your eyes, but only a few will catch your heart.
- There are two sides of every question.
- There is "no" difference between "Table" and "Notable".
- There is a proverb in Tamil which says "You go and sit under a palm tree and drink the best drink/milk, the passerby will still think you are drinking toddy".
- There is ache only as long as there is head.
- There is no condition in grace.
- There is no cosmetic for beauty like happiness.

Be a good global citizen, say no to tobacco.

- There is no escape from death.
- There is no fall more painful than to fall from the heaven.
- There is no one in this world who does not like being appreciated.
- There is no one who can be above criticism. There is no way of pleasing everyone.
- There is no right or wrong, except "Culture" that makes it so.
- There is no right way to do something wrong.
- There is no Team Spirit only Spirit.
- There is only one pretty child in the world, and every mother has it.
- There was a time when petrol outlets were called "service stations". Now "Self-service" is often the order of the day.
- They are Mad(e) for each other.
- They are true friends. They work together. That's why there is a key to every lock.
- They say we should pay tax with a smile, I tried, but they settle only for money.
- Those who listen, will accept the truth.
- Though cattle are of different colours, the milk yielded by them is of the same colour (white).
- Throw out something everyday.

Staying away from tobacco.

- To deny all, is to confess all.
- To teach is to learn twice.
- Today many of us cannot have a garden like that of grandmother's but we can surely keep a few plants, indoors. These will brighten up the house, absorb mells, and help purifying the air.
- Today, we have more information about sex than our forefathers ever had. But today, most of the people worry about sex.
- Too many cooks spoil the broth. But many hands make work light.
- Too much in circulation makes the price go down. Create value through scarcity.
- Travelling on foot has always been of great value.
- Truth conquers, and lie falls.
- Truth does not have to follow the rules.
- Truth has no contradiction.
- Truth is the first casualty in the game of politics.
- Try not to do too many things at once.
- Try to say NO to make YES more powerful.
- Two wrongs do not make a right, then you must try three.
- United, there is little that we can not do. Divided, there is little that we can do.

If you can not stop smoking, cancer will.

Use of the Telephone: Sometimes the only early point for Relationship.

- Var Vadhu is now War Vadhu.
- Vasudeva Kutumbakam (Universal brotherhood).

This slogan is also written at the entrance gate of the Parliament.

- Vehicle number plate is not a style or status Symbol. Delhi Police is prosecuting vehicles with defective Number Plates.
- WANTED: A Vivekananda.
- *Waqt Har Din Suraj Ko Bhi Duba Deta Hai.*
- War makes History.
- Waste not, want not.
- We are all branded with a religion whereas even religion says: God is one.
- We are efficient in excuse.
- We are with you always and in all ways.
- We boil at different points.
- We can be 100% sure that we will die.
- We change our honesty according to our interest.
- We changed the name of seeds to beans so that you may eat it.
- We communicate our ego but do not communicate with the person.

Smoking! You must be joking.

- We feel tired while standstill.
- We find it to be in extremely bad taste for individuals to boast of their accomplishments; but when countries do so we call it "National pride".
- We go by the philosophy "Tomorrow never comes" but it is better to remember that "Tomorrow never dies".
- We love the cuckoo and look down the crow, whereas the cuckoo grows up in the crow's nest.
- We make love secretly but fight wars openly.
- We must not judge higher things from a lower standpoint.
- We quite often change jobs, friends and what not, but not ourselves.
- We seldom give thanks to wife for good dishes but shout within a short time if a pinch of salt is excess or less in any dish.
- We shed tears to secure a job, but refuse to sweat when we get one.
- We soon believe what we desire.
- We still hire sporting ground for marriages.
- We tend to judge people by our own standards.

A smoking parents too bears a heavy responsibility for their childs health.

- Whatever man's mind can conceive and believe, it can achieve.
- What I learned on my own I still remember.
- What is fashion to one wanting clothes?
- What the daughter-in-law loves, the mother-in-law hates?
- What the eye does not see, the heart does not grieve over.
- What you cannot avoid, welcome.
- Whatever affects the whole, affects the parts also. Just as when a tree is shaken, its branches and other parts are also shaken. When the tree falls, the monkey scatters.
- Whatever you speak good or bad, speak cleverly.
- When anger arises, think of the consequence.
- When children stand still, they have done some ill.
- When everything seems lost, remember, future remains.
- When friends meet, heart is warmed.
- When home is sweet all is sweet.
- When I asked a minister "If you will be made Chief Minister. How you will act ?" He said: "*Mere*

Smoke away your worries, not your lungs.

Pairon Main Ghoonghroo Bandha De To Phir Meri Chall Dekh Le."

- When in doubt, ask when not in doubt.
- When one is thirsty, can one sit idle?
- When prayers go up, blessings come down.
- When someone starts a sentence with "simply", you should expect to hear something very complicated.
- When the principle of pleasing others is followed, then everything, whether right or wrong, may be done.
- When we take life seriously, it is easy. But if we do not take it seriously, it becomes serious.
- When you dial a wrong number, you never get an engaged tone.
- Where there is a cause, there is an effect. Where there is moon there is its pleasing lust.
- Where there is truth, there is knowledge.
- Where there is smoke, there is pollution.
- Whole life we give health and earn wealth and after retirement we give wealth to earn health.
- William Shakespeare, English playwright, could not find a suitable title for a play. So he called it "As You Like It".

Earlier cancer is detected, the earlier it can be treated and cured.

- Win or lose is at your hand and not at the hands of fate.
- Winning is earning, losing is learning.
- Winning is not everything. It is the only thing.
- Without a change in your behaviour, just saying, "I am sorry" is not enough.
- Women dress to please men and displease other women.
- Women should use perfume in a "mute mode". Sufficient to know it is there, but not to over power everyone around.
- Wonderful – sometimes wonder, sometimes fool.
- Words out of mouth fly on wings.
- Work for a cause and not for applause.
- Work hard, that's the bottom line.
- Work joyfully and peacefully. Work moves mountains.
- Work never gets you tired. It is the essence of work which makes you tired.
- Work teaches how to work.
- Work with integrity and succeed with integrity that is missing today.
- World is an ocean of misery.
- Wrist is stronger than five fingers together.

You can stop smoking. Only you can.

- X-ray of handsome person is also ugly.
- *Yad Bhavam, Tad Bhavati* (you become, what you think).
- Yes, I have taken a decision not to take decision.
- You are guaranteed a repetition when you hear the declaration "never again!"
- You are never old to take a dance class.
- You can judge a man by what he laughs at.
- You may not be helpful but you must not be harmful.
- You must do the important, but delegate the urgent.
- You must learn from your past mistakes, but not lean on your past success.
- You must stick to your conviction, but be ready to abandon your assumptions.
- You must think like high-tech, must act like a high-touch firm.
- You must understand that seeing is believing, but also know that believing is seeing.
- You never get a second chance to make the first impression.
- You remember e-mails you sent that were not answered better than e-mails that you did not answer.

Destroy tobacco before it destroys you.

- You show me the man, I will show you the rule.
- Your competitor is yourself.
- Your name is "yours" but is used mostly by others i.e. yours faithfully.
- Your present is because of your past, and your future depends upon your present.
- Your reputation is harmed the most by what you say to defend it.
- Your reputation runs faster than you.
- Your smile is right under your nose.
- Youth looks ahead, old age looks back, middle age looks worried.
- Zen Quotes : When the character of a man is not clear to you, look at his friends.

"WORDS OF WISDOM"

- A country can be judged by the quality of its proverb.
- A democracy without discipline is a democracy without a future.
- A friend of mine spent twenty years looking for the perfect woman, unfortunately, when he found her, he discovered that she was looking for the perfect man.
- A golden rule is that there are no golden rules.
- A good customer is one who purchases quality wisely not quantity cheaply; much bar-gainers can never do justice to be a worthy customer.

Surrogate tobacco ads may be banned.

- A good denial is the best point in law.
- A good opportunity is seldom presented, and is easily lost.
- A happy family is a healthy family.
- A house can't be kept without talk.
- A law is that which cannot be broken.
- A leader is the one who can create more leaders.
- A lie is more believable than a truth.
- A light heart lives long.
- A man cannot be too careful in the choice of his enemies!
- A man is not honest simply because he never had a chance to steal.
- A man who does not plan long ahead will find trouble right at his door.
- A man without a smiling face must not open a shop.
- A mouse does not rely on just one hole.
- A needle is not sharp at both ends.
- A person who is not disciplined cannot be cautioned.
- A public-opinion poll is no substitute for thought.
- A reverse side also has a reverse side.
- A rich man has no need of character.

A number of studies have shown that tobacco use is a significant factor in miscarriages among pregnant smokers, and that it contributes to a number of other threats to the health of the foetus.

- A rose too often smelled loses its fragrance.
- A smile is the best lighting system of the face, the best cooling system of the head and the warming system of the heart. Keep Smiling!
- A snake deserves no pity.
- A son is a son till he takes him a wife, a daughter is a daughter all her life.
- A thing well said will be wit in all languages.
- A wise man will make more opportunities than he finds.
- A woman can hide her love for 40 years, but her disgust and anger not even for one day.
- A woman is charming and beautiful if she is appreciated by a man, otherwise it has no meaning.
- About 68% want to change their job only because of their manager's attitude. "My boss is worst" is a common feeling : Survey.
- Accounting is the language of business.
- After all, if India wins as a nation, all of us will be winners – the best win-win situation.
- After any salary raise, you will have less money at the end of the month than you did before.
- All men's miseries derive from not being able to sit quietly in a room alone.
- All of us, at sometime or the other, have to do a job that we don't like. It's a universal truth and will remain an eternal truth.

Although as smoking causes a greater increase of the risk of cancer than cigar smoking, cigar smokers still have an increased risk for many health problems, including cancer, when compared to non-smokers.

- All strangers are in relation to each other.
- All weapons are useless, if you are not inspired to fight.
- Always be smarter than the people who hire you.
- Always cultivate the heart.
- Always magnify the plus points and add them in your memory span and ignore the minus points, keep them in forgetting record, people will worship you.
- Always mistrust a subordinate who never finds fault with his superior.
- Always take liability as asset, always look towards the best, always be honest in your efforts and always be clear in your vision.
- An angry man opens his mouth and shuts his eyes.
- Anger can be an expensive luxury.
- Anxiety does not help. One should not worry excessively. At best bow before Almighty.
- Any ailment, however trivial, will deduct your happiness.
- Any citizen following any faith has the fundamental right to live happily.
- Any tool, when dropped, will roll to the least accessible corner of the room.
- Anything that can't go on forever will end.
- Anything that happens once does not necessarily happen again, everything that happens twice is likely to happen for the third time as well.

- Anything will fit a naked man.
- As the saying goes, "Never give your opponent a second chance, you may not survive the counter attack!"
- As we advance in life, we learn the limits of our abilities.
- As we live, so we learn.
- Avoid being artificial.
- A dream without action is useless and an action without dream is a nightmare.
- A lie might have save one for a day, but turn him a liar forever.
- A migrating person grows healthy, wealthy and wise.
- A rolling stone gathers no moss – but it gets to see places.
- All good things must come to an end – while bad things seldom seem to end.
- Always complaining against others is not good. In facts, the complaining attitude is a very poor attitude for a human being and many people have this complaining attitude.
- Arriving at the first solution to a problem may not always be the best-suited one.
- Assumptions are the result of laziness and lack of interest.
- Bad is never good until worse happens.
- Barking dogs seldom bite – others, you being an exception.

"Beware of Smoking" (An Earnest Request).

- Beauty is skin deep.
- Be fair.
- Be silent, or say something better than silence.
- Be sure your sin will find it out.
- Beauty needs no ornaments.
- Because something is a 'fashion' does not mean that it is bad, unsuitable or unnecessary. If it makes sense, adopt the model. If it does not make sense, then ignore the fashion.
- Because something is good and useful does not mean that it has the same value in all circumstances.
- Before doing any task or taking any decision one should be reasonable and legal minded.
- Before you score you must have a goal.
- Being in power is not a blessing. It is a curse. It's a very heavy responsibility.
- Being in the right camp, rather rightly doing one's duty continues to be the necessity for nearness to boss or the power center.
- Better a red face than a black heart.
- Better a true enemy than a false friend.
- Beware : some liars tell the truth.
- Birds of a feather flock together – especially when they have a common grouse.
- Blessings do not come in pairs; misfortunes never come singly.
- Boss, with the limited exceptions, continues to be a dreaded animal.

Cancer – Battling all odds.

- Breasts are sisters, not twins!
- Business first : pleasure afterwards.
- But eradicating corruption is not enough to sustain a country.
- By definition, tradition means no change.
- By reading books, we become parrots.
- Caste is a football in the political game.
- Challenge is never, never, never an attack.
- Chanakya also respected his enemies. His advice was, "He should enter the enemy's residence with permission".
- Change is the law of life. And those who look only to the past or present are certain to miss the future.
- Chankaya says, If there is equal advancement in peace or war, we should resort to peace.
- Character development is not just a matter of one day.
- Cheats never prosper – but they do get rich fast.
- Check the wants; wants are endless.
- "Cheque enclosed" are the two most beautiful words in the English language.
- Choose neither a woman nor linen by candlelight.
- Conquering the world through speech.

Cancer begins & ends with people.

- CONGRATULATIONS – sugar coated envy.
- Corruption - The 2011 corruption perception index measures the perceived levels of public sector corruption in 183 countries and territories around the world.
- Corruption is the abuse of entrusted power for private gain. It hurts everyone who depend on the integrity of people in a position of authority.
- Courage goes all the ways.
- Courtiers are courtiers, everywhere.
- Cowards don't make history.
- Custom reconciles us to everything.
- Daughter, I'm telling you. O daughter-in-law, listen to this.....
- Death always comes too early or too late.
- Death does not ask a person for permission prior to arrival, nor does it give one an early warning about its being on its way. Death comes in ways that we do not expect.
- Dead men tell no tales – only their biographers do.
- Death is a great leveller – though life is seldom a level playground.
- Death means only a change of garments.
- Death pays all debts.
- Decentralization may lead to simplicity in operation but increased complexity in administration.

Cancer is not one disease but many diseases.

- Delegation, in practice, often pertains to shifting of what is difficult and inconvenient.
- Deliver your words not by number but by weight.
- Difficulties vanish when faced boldly.
- Disappointment's cousin is frustration.
- Discontent is the first step in the progress of man or a nation.
- Distant hills look beautiful; near ones are ugly.
- Divide the fire and you will soon put it out.
- Do not act humble. Be humble.
- Do not be afraid to make mistakes.
- Do not be chaotic in your life.
- Do not be shaken by hardship.
- Do not consult only one person. Do not consult too many people. Consult with the mature.
- Do not expect gratitude from anyone.
- Do not laugh excessively, for verily, excessive laughter kills the heart.
- Do not let horoscopes influence you.
- Do not listen to the voice of the mind. Listen to the voice of the heart. Mind weavers; heart does not falter. Mind fears; heart is not daunted. Mind is the house of doubts, reasoning and theories; heart when purified, becomes the dwelling of Beloved God.
- Do not respond to an injurious statement that is made about you.

Doctors treat disease and also people.

- Doing good to others gives comfort to the heart. The first person who benefits from an act of charity is the benefactor himself, by seeing changes in himself and in his manners, by finding peace, by watching a smile form on the lips of another person.
- Doing ordinary things at an ordinary time could give you extra-ordinary results.
- Doing things slowly helps the mind to clarify and simplify things. It is a form of meditation.
- Don't accept my words, simply because they are my words. Accept but only after duly examining them with reason. Believe in yourself only then you can be a torchbearer to yourself.
- Don't buy the house; buy the neighborhood.
- Don't judge a man by the words of his mother; listen to the comments of his neighbours.
- Dreaming is our only right.
- Dreams seldom materialize on their own.
- During the British Raj, many believed that our colony was governed by a "Divide and Rule" policy. Sardar Vallabhbhai Patel, our first Home Minister and Deputy Prime Minister, had a different opinion. He said, "We divide ourselves, and they rule."
- During the days when our former President A.P.J. Kalam was creating missiles, he was asked why he was creating weapons of destruction. He replied, "Only strength will respect strength".

Environmental tobacco smoke exposure and maternal smoking during pregnancy have been shown to cause lower infant birth weights.

- Duty is seldom sweet.
- Each Year is a new year.
- Eat and drink with your relatives; do business with strangers.
- Eat at pleasure, drink by measure.
- Education is a better safeguard of liberty than a standing army.
- Elections determine who is in power, but they do not determine how power is used.
- Electorates tend to get the politicians they deserve.
- Empty vessels make the most sound – and are promptly heard.
- English is seen as a threat to Hindi or other local languages.
- Entire confusion in the world is within yourself, if you recognize yourself very well, there is no confusion in the world.
- Earning money and spending it for one self is not labha (profit).
- Errors are not acceptable but the search for ultimate perfection may add more complexity than it is worth.
- Even a correct decision when taken too late, is wrong.
- Even a hare will insult the dead lion.

Events are planned in a number of countries to mark World No Tobacco Day. Many of the events are aimed at persuading people, especially the young, not to start smoking. Others aim to educate people about the many health benefits of quitting.

- Even a one eyed guy will wink at a beautiful woman.
- Even the prayers of an ant reach to heaven.
- Every boss has a boss above him.
- Every country should set up a National Institute for Simplicity.
- Every day do something that will inch you closer to a better tomorrow.
- Every disadvantage has its advantage, (Every dark cloud has a silver lining).
- Every great achievement is done slowly.
- Every head has its own headache.
- Every little thing counts in a crisis.
- Every stream has its source. (The only thing in the universe that has no source or origin is the Supreme Power, which has always existed and has no beginning and no end).
- Everybody wants to be something; nobody wants to grow.
- Everyone excels in something in which another fails.
- Everything can be improved.
- Everything looks useful till you buy it.
- Everything on earth marches forward.
- Everything that has gentleness in it is beautified.
- Everything that is done in the world is done by hope.

Evidence suggests that non-smokers are up to twice as likely as smokers to develop Parkinson's disease or Alzheimer's disease.

- Everywhere is He. He is everything. He is in everything.
- Extract the honey but do not break the hive. When the bee lands on a flower (doing so for a practical purpose) it does not destroy it.
- Failures are the must in life, so never get disheartened, but always learn from failures and be careful that the same failures may not be repeated.
- Faith is the greatest remedy.
- Fear can make a donkey attack a lion.
- Fear those who are afraid of you.
- FLAME : Financial Literacy Agenda for Mass Empowerment.
- Flies never visit an egg that has no crack.
- For a new beginning. Go back to new beginning.
- For example – is not proof.
- Forecasts usually tell us more of the forecaster than of the forecast.
- Former President A.P.J. Abdul Kalam puts it, "It is the wings of fire that gives you the ability to reach out to the skies."
- Generosity is key to a happy marriage.
- Give even an onion graciously.
- Give the world the best you have, and it may never be enough. Give the world the best you have anyway.

To say you're only smoking half a pack instead of two a day is good, but it is better to say that "I have stopped smoking" and STOP.

- God's best gift to us is not things but opportunities.
- Good work done is not enough for fair reward and assignments.
- Great & Good are seldom the same man.
- Great things come from the heart.
- Green is the prime colour of the world, and that from which its loveliness arises.
- Habit is the 6th sense that overrules the other 5.
- Hanging a 'WELCOME' or a 'SALE ON' is not everything. You have to also maintain a homely atmosphere which will make customers feel welcome and, the first step towards this is to clean up your act.
- Happiness shared is happiness multiplied.
- Happiness does not buy you money.
- Happy is the man who can make a living by his hobby.
- Hatred is never ended by hatred, but by love.
- Have you ever seen a sign on a road reading: "This is not the road to the airport."
- He makes no friends who never made a foe.
- He that is afraid to shake the dice will never throw a six.
- He who is always afraid of loss always loses.
- He who knows nothing, doubts nothing.
- He who serves two masters has to lie to one.
- Heroism is the result of true sacrifice.

Support 100% smoke-free public places.

- Hobby keeps boredom away.
- Honesty is the best policy – where others are concerned.
- Honesty, often, is not the best policy for trouble free and efficient corporate dealings.
- Hope is a waking dream.
- How many will listen to the truth when you tell them?
- Humour can cure any malady.
- Hunting is not a sport. In a sport, both sides should know they're in the game.
- Hurt me with the truth......But never comfort me with a lie.
- I am a better investor because I am a businessman and a better businessman because I am an investor.
- I can accept failure; but I can't accept not trying.
- I do not know who my grandfather was. I am now more concern to know his grandson will be.
- I don't know what the future may hold, but I know who holds the future.
- I don't try to jump over seven-foot bars; I look around for one-foot bars that I can step over.
- I have cancer but cancer does not have me.
- I light my candles from their torches.

Medical researchers have found that smoking is a predictor of divorce. Smokers have a 53% greater chance of divorce than non-smokers.

- I made my life monument.
- I make it a practice to laugh in order to give rest and comfort to my heart.
- I put my mind above the bar and then my body followed.
- I see God in every human being.
- I was angered, for I had no shoes. Then I met a man who had no feet.
- I've never let my school interfere with my education.
- If a link is broken, the whole chain breaks.
- If at first you do succeed, quit trying.
- If I love myself, I love you. If I love you, I love myself.
- If luck comes, who comes not? If luck comes not, who comes?
- If observation and belief failed to tally, it was the belief that was deemed to be wrong rather than what was observed.
- If principles become dated they are no longer principles.
- If something is not a problem it does not get any thinking time.
- If the patient dies, the doctor has killed him, but if he gets well, the saints have saved him.
- If the rich could hire other people to die for them, the poor could make a wonderful living.

Most smokers, when denied access to nicotine, exhibit symptoms such as irritability, jitteriness, dry mouth, and rapid heartbeat.

- If you are kind, people may accuse you of selfish motives: Be kind anyway.
- If you are successful, you will win some false friends and some true enemies.
- If you be a winner in life, buy a book, read a book, gift a book and talk of a book, as they are the best friends, philosophers and guide of men, they are the windows through the soul look out, they are for leisure and pleasure, they develop and make us knowledgeable and beneficial in all respect.
- If you blink, they score. If you go for a pee, they score three times. During TV break, there is a penalty shot.
- If you deal in camel, make the doors high.
- If you don't make mistakes, you can't make decisions.
- If you let yourself be undisciplined on the small things, you will probably be undisciplined on the large things as well.
- If you look for problems you will end up playing the blame game. Instead, define a purpose for your organisation and its people. Most of us are problem finders. Change this mindset and cultivate a goal-oriented approach. As Gandhiji said, "Find a purpose, the means will follow."
- If you need a 'rainbow', then you have to face the 'rain' also.

No Smoking is an advice ere evoking.

- If you really cannot do something, leave it.
- If you really have nothing to say, it is better to make it as complex as possible otherwise people will see that nothing is being said.
- If you think you're leading and no one is following you, then you're only taking a walk.
- If you want good service, serve yourself.
- If you want to be a rebel, be kind.
- Imagination is more important than knowledge. Knowledge is limited. Imagination encircles the world.
- Imagination is the eye of the soul.
- Imitation is suicide.
- In a difficult business, no sooner is one problem solved than another surfaces – never is there just one cockroach in the kitchen.
- In about the same degree as you are helpful, you will be happy.
- In any work, problems are unavoidable. It only ends when we are in the grave.
- In India, we consider the scriptures to be mirrors.
- In looking for someone to hire, you look for three qualities: integrity, intelligence, and energy. But the most important is integrity, because if they don't have that, the other two qualities, intelligence and energy, are going to kill you.
- In looking for someone to hire, you look for three qualities: integrity, intelligence, and energy.

No Smoking, No Provoking. Use of Hooka can be as detrimental to health as smoking cigarette.

But the most important is integrity, because if they don't have that, the other two qualities, intelligence and energy, are going to kill you.

- In the entire process of human development, the most important stage is the grooming and education of early childhood (2-1/2 to 5 years) which is the psychologically based foundation on which building or structure of the whole personality stands.
- In the Upanishads, a student asks the teacher, "Why does the evil win?" The Guru replied, "because the good are not united".
- Inform me of a man's determination and I will tell you what kind of man he is.
- Injustice all around is justice!
- Instructions for machines, computers, etc., are always written by those who know the system and are not much help to those who do not.
- Intellectual brilliance is no guarantee against being dead wrong.
- Internal politics and personal agenda often play an important role in corporate governance.
- Invest in the 'generation-next'.
- It is a recession when your neighbour loses his job. It is a depression when you lose yours.
- It is a very sad thing that nowadays there is so little useless information.

No Smoking, Good Invoking. Tobacco use is the top cause of deaths worldwide.

- It is better to be born a beggar than a fool.
- It is better to marry and repent than not to marry and regret.
- It is by doubting that we come to investigate and by investigating that we recognise the truth.
- It is easier to abstain than to restrain.
- It is easier to stay out of trouble than it is to get out of trouble.
- It is good to be born a child but bad to remain a child.
- It is never too late to give up your prejudices.
- It is not necessary to do extraordinary things to get extraordinary results.
- It is not the knowing that is difficult, but the doing.
- It is the knowledge of wealth and a wealth of knowledge.
- It is the neglect of timely repair that makes rebuilding necessary.
- It makes no difference whether the product is cars or cosmetics. A company is only as good as the people it keeps.
- It may be better to simplify a process rather than train people to cope with the complexity.
- It takes twenty years to build a reputation and five minutes to lose it. If you think about that you will do things differently.

Refrain from smoking, remain well evoking.

- It was management guru Stephen Covey who first coined the term 'win win situation'. Now it is commonly used terminology in the corporate world. It is a paradigm shift in management thinking, based on the principle of 'live and let live'.
- It's easier to resist at the beginning than at the end.
- It's hard to teach a young dog old tricks.
- It's the 'law' of gravity which holds people onto planet earth? If this law was missing, then everything would be out of control.
- Jealousy is not something new.
- Just because your ratings are bigger doesn't mean you're better.
- Justifying a fault doubles it.
- Knowledge is the costliest valuable thing in the world, which we wish to obtain in no cost, no expenditure, but in donation or in begging even.
- Knowledge is the edge.
- Law is uniform.
- Learn from your losses, you paid for them.
- Life is like a game of chess, changing with each move.
- Life is for one generation; a good name is forever.

Show the truth. Picture Warnings Save Lives.

- Life is tragedy for those who feel, and a comedy for those who think.
- Life is variable.
- Let's work hard now so that we can sleep peacefully later.
- Like attracts like.
- Like fingerprints, all marriages are different.
- Love is a serious mental disease.
- Love is as strong as death.
- Love your neighbour, yet pull not your hedge.
- Make haste slowly.
- Make sure you have a different opinion and people will talk about you.
- Marrying for money is probably a bad idea under any circumstances, but it is absolutely nuts if you are already rich.
- Men's best successes come after their disappointments.
- Merit and skills of a junior are often perceived as threat.
- Migration does not automatically convert people into assets in the new place.
- Money never starts an idea. It is always the idea that starts the money.
- Money only makes you what you already are.
- Most people do not open their eyes to the beauty of the nature, but open them only to gold or silver.

Smoke, or any partially burnt organic matter, contains carcinogens (cancer- causing agents).

- Most people get interested in stocks when everyone else is. The time to get interested is when no one else is. You can't buy what is popular and do well.
- Much coin, much care.
- My brain – It's my second favourite organ.
- My idea of a group decision is to look in the mirror.
- Never follow unknowns, short-cuts, temporary gains and misleading decisions, as these may ruin you totally.
- Nightingale got no prize at the poultry show.
- No man can stand at the top because he is put there.
- No sweet without sweat.
- Nobody's sweetheart is ugly.
- Not all developing countries are the same.
- Not having a headache is the most important wish in the world when you have a severe headache.
- Nothing happens unless first a dream.
- Obstacles are great incentives.
- Old age does not announce itself..... (Old age will advance, without efforts, on us gradually, whether we like it or not).

Smoke-free walk. Tobacco is the single greatest cause of preventable death globally.

- On the day of victory no one is tired.
- On the evening of the big date, a pimple appears on your nose.
- Once, the leader of successful organisation was asked how the company managed to maintain its good performance even after the Founder had passed away. He replied, "The master is gone, but he left behind masterpieces!"
- One ounce of good luck is better than a ton of brains.
- One song can inspire many, one flower can give fragrant climate, one candle can bring light, one smile can begin friendship and one life can make the difference.
- One step at a time.
- One who has control over his pants, hand and mouth has nothing to worry about.
- One who is allowed to sin, sin less.
- Only if the fear of punishment exists, will there be discipline and peace in society. No one desires war. But, at times, it is unavoidable. War against terrorism is talk of the world.
- Opportunity often comes disguised in the form of misfortune, or temporary defeat.
- Our computer does not actually do anything. We just blame it for everything.
- Our legal system has made life too easy for criminals and too difficult for the law abiding citizens : Supreme Court.

Smokers are three times as likely to die before the age of 60 or 70 as non-smokers.

- Our life is like a pre-paid card with limited validity.
- Our offerings please God according to our zeal and not according to their value.
- Our society respects power, not excellence or integrity. The lion is always right and the lion's friends have a good life.
- Parkinson's Law stated that "work expands to fill the time allotted to it".
- Past is the cancelled cheque, present is the cash money and future is the promissory note, decide what you require?
- Peace begins with a smile.
- Peace of mind is in having the basic necessities of life.
- People are judged by their residential addresses.
- People ask you for criticism, but they only want praise.
- People do not kick a dead dog.
- People do not leave organisations, they leave their bosses.
- People who are not very good at having new ideas might be very good at indicating where new ideas are badly needed. They pin-point areas which need simplifying/new thinking.

Smokers often report that cigarettes help relieve feelings of stress. Users report feelings of relaxation, sharpness, calmness, and alertness. Those new to smoking may experience nausea, dizziness and rapid heartbeat.

- People who are resting on their laurels are wearing them on the wrong end.
- People who have nothing to say are never at a loss of words.
- Perseverance is king.
- Personal consideration and other elements of narrowness, rather than consensus, are often the basis of decision making.
- Poetry is vocal painting, as painting is silent poetry.
- Poor men's words have little weight.
- Poverty is no sin, but terribly inconvenient.
- Power does strange things to people, it is said, but when they go out of power even stranger things can happen.
- Practice is absolutely necessary.
- Prayers should always be short and sincere.
- Price is what you pay, value is what you get.
- Problems and challenges are the essential ingredients of life, face them courageously, patiently, and calmly with a hope to get positive and acceptable solutions.
- Proper words in proper places make the true definition of a style.
- Purity is strength.
- Quality is not an act, it is a habit.

Smokers report higher levels of everyday stress.

- Remember, a sculptor always makes a six inch model before the actual 60-foot statue!
- Remember, the king men are stronger than the king!
- Research shows that 95 per cent of people do not use 90 per cent of the features on their video-recorders – because they are too complicated.
- Respect elder and aged people because you can learn a lot from their long experiences, life style and skills which may be pleasurable, achievement oriented or troublesome so sort out very economically what you can adopt for your betterment and what you can ignore for your peaceful life.
- Respect time and you will earn respect from the world.
- Richness is when you need no more.
- Risk comes from not knowing what you are doing.
- Rule No.1 : Never lose money. Rule No. 2 : Never forget rule No.
- Satisfaction is richness and safety.
- See with your mind; hear with your heart.
- SEVA means serving earnestly, voluntarily and ambitiously for the welfare of whole humanity but it is very pinching that a country which has no culturally rich heritage of SEVA throughout the world is now levelled as Seva or Service Tax

Smoking causes impotence because it promotes arterial narrowing.

on the one hand and publicity of Seva works on the other hand.

- Seven trades and luck is lost.
- Several excuses are always less convincing than one.
- Silence is a lot to articulate than noise, for those who have achieved the silence; they might use it as a language for the benefit of the society, for betterment communicability, for better expression of one's potentialities and for giving forceful messages and preaching to the masses.
- Silence is medication for sorrow.
- Silence is often advantageous.
- Simplicity is elegant.
- Simplicity makes life simpler. However, finding a simpler way is usually neither simple nor easy.
- Size does not matter, planning does.
- Small men think they are small; great men never know they are great.
- Small mistakes are not small if committed by people at the top.
- So many of our dreams at first seem impossible, then they seem improbable, and then, when we summon the will, they soon become inevitable.
- Some people talk in their sleep. Lecturers talk while other people sleep.
- Someone is sitting in the shade today because someone planted a tree a long time ago.

Smoking has become a fashion, it's true, not a joke.
Even while standing, sitting, sleeping, talking, and walking.

- Spiritual values are like a ray of sunlight in the lives of India's citizens.
- Spiritualism is different from religion, the former unites whereas the latter divides, so in order to bring spirituality in life, we have to worship our Almighty, may be God, Allah, Vishnu, Shiva, Krishna, Rama, Jesus Christ, or thousands of names by our means and styles but with a feeling of complete.
- Start taking small decisions.
- Stay in the company of the righteous.
- Successful people do not relax in chairs, they relax in work.
- Sunshine all the time makes a desert.
- There are three kinds of people – first, those who do not start work because of the fear of obstacles. Second, those who start, but stop when they face obstacles. And, third, those who work inspite of obstacles and overcome it.
- To love and to be loved is the greatest achievement of life.
- To have a friend, you need to be a friend first.
- Teach your child to hold his tongue; he will learn fast enough to speak.
- Teacher should develop the language and communication skills properly; he should be a good listener, effective speaker, sharp reader and commendable writer and translate the various

Smoking is an addiction everywhere provoking.

theoretical concepts into practical illustrations.

- Tell me and I'll forget, show me and I may remember, involve me and I'll understand.
- Temper is a funny thing; you can't get rid of it by losing it.
- The bathroom mirror steams up exactly when you need it.
- The best of you is the one who is best with his family and I am the best of you to his family.
- The best sauce for food is hunger.
- The best way to make your dreams come true is to wake up.
- The blessings of pain – In the history of the world there are those who have produced their greatest works due to the pain and suffering that they experienced.
- The boards squeak loudest when you need to be quietest.
- The body says what words cannot.
- The book is the best companion that does not praise you and does not entice you to evil.
- The coffin is the brother of the cradle.
- The constant friend is never welcomed.
- The corruption of the best-things gives rise to the worst.
- The coward dies many deaths and the brave man dies one.

Smoking is harmful to health. It is mere waste of wealth.

- The deaf have no enemies.
- The dream of a cat is filled with mice.
- The easiest person to deceive is one's self.
- The fact that people are full of greed, fear or folly is predictable. The sequence is not predictable.
- The first duty of love is to listen.
- The first idea that comes to mind may not be so interesting but the second and third ideas that flow from it can be very interesting. Love at first sight but it is better to have a second look.
- The first time it is a favour; the second time a rule.
- The greatest power that a person possesses is the power to choose.
- The Internet lives where anyone can access it.
- The investor of today does not profit from yesterday's growth.
- The job of central bank is to worry.
- The lazier a person is, the more likely is that person to seek simpler ways to do things.
- The longer the night lasts, the more our dreams will be.
- The man behind the machine is more important than the machine.
- The man who knows it can't be done counts the risk, not the reward.
- The mind that is anxious about future events is miserable.

Smoking is harmful to the ovaries, potentially causing female infertility, and the degree of damage is dependent upon the amount and length of time a woman smokes.

- The monarchy is the oldest profession in the world.
- The more corrupt the state, the more numerous the laws.
- The most beautiful and fascinating objects in this universe cannot be seen with naked eyes but can be felt only with the heart.
- The only way to keep yourself productive is by having at least a month's work in front of you.
- The past is gone forever. This is because the past is non-existence.
- The poor sleep soundly.
- The power of man has grown in every sphere, except over himself.
- The purpose of a rule may be to remind us of what lies behind that rule.
- The purpose should be bigger than you and me.
- The real problem is what to do with problem solvers after the problem is solved.
- The right answer to a fool is silence.
- The secret of success is to know something nobody else knows.
- The sleepless nights I spend in learning the sciences, are more beloved to me than other things.
- The son-in-law's sack is never full.
- The soul desire more if you encourage it, but returns to contentment when it is disciplined.

Smoking is ugly. Tobacco - Killing Me Softly.

- The standard of life is even more significant than the standard of living.
- The subject interesting to the teacher will bore the students.
- The sun will set without the assistance.
- The teacher said – don't be serious, be sincere.
- The time is always right to do what is right.
- The tongue says various things because it has no bone.
- The value of achievement lies in the achieving.
- The view point of life should be changed like two days one night (more lights), not one day two nights (more darkness) so the way of life will automatically be changed.
- The way you cut your meat reflects the way you live.
- The wife of today tries to look superior, but does not know how to wear her sari properly.
- The world is not a problem, the problem is your unawareness.
- The world's a bubble and the life of man less than span.
- The year does nothing else but open and shut.
- The years teach much which the days never know.
- There are no national frontiers to learning.
- There is a huge difference between the business that grows and requires lots of capital to do so and the business that grows and doesn't require capital.

"Smoking is Prohibited", Ubiquitously Exhibited!

- There is a time for all things.
- There is an old saying in the army, "Your success in war depends on your preparation during peace.
- There is an old saying "Well begun is half done." It is a bad one. I would use instead – "Not begun at all until half done."
- There is no education like adversity.
- There is no medicine for suspicion in the world, because this is a disease based on faulty and irrational part of one's polluted mind.
- There is no medicine like hope, there is no tonic like expectation, there is no therapy like encouragement and there is no treatment like emotional showering.
- There is no way to peace, peace is the way.
- There is not a single problem that does not have a solution.
- There is nothing more deadly than a feeling of inferiority.
- They can because they think they can.
- They know enough who know how to learn.
- Think before they think – that is the rule of warfare.
- Think something positive, listen something meaningful, say something worthwhile, do something concrete and feel something sentimental.
- This body is for service to others.

Smoking was powerfully implicated in the causation of lung cancer. Cigarette can only be a perfect killer and nothing else.

- Though, we are very negative in thinking and action but we are not cautious about the negative, damaging, destructive and killing aspects of life.
- Through the heart comes inspiration.
- Time is a physician which heels every grief.
- Time is infinite.
- To be free – keep your mouth shut.
- To have more, desire less.
- To succeed in any project, the key to success is silence.
- To teach is to learn twice.
- To weep is a sign of weakness of bondage.
- Today will become yesterday by tomorrow.
- Too often I find that the volume of paper expands to fill the available briefcases.
- Training is for the future, musical instruments denote inspiration, while signals denote communication.
- Truth is often unpleasant often tried to boss or seniors in an unfiltered manner.
- Truth is tough.
- Truth that causes the heart to be opened and a falsehood that causes it to harden.
- Turnarounds seldom turn.
- Use power to curb power.

> ***"Giving up smoking is the easiest thing in the world. I know because I've done it thousands of times."***

- Use time efficiently and concentrate all of your efforts on achieving something today by improving your manners, taking care of your health, and improving your relations with others.
- Usually we are running for nothing and throwing of everything which we already possess. If you laugh at yourself, there is nobody in the universe to dare to laugh on yourself, therefore try to laugh or make fun of yourself and become the great.
- View things from a spiritual angle.
- Violence is pollution and pollution is violence.
- We all have problems and so we are always in search of solutions. Don't go anywhere, solutions lie within.
- We are not creature of circumstance, we are creators of circumstance.
- We are the music makers, and we are the dreamers of dreams.
- We have to learn from others.
- We Indians are here, there, everywhere. No matter how much others love us or hate us, there is absolutely no way anyone can ignore us.
- We learn little from our success, but a lot from our failures.
- We make more enemies by what we say than friends by what we do.
- We make our fortune, and we call it fate.

"Smoking kills. If you're killed, you've lost a very important part of your life."

- We normally do not care and love those who are near around us but always bother for those who are not around us.
- We refer to our country as "Mother India", but hardly allow her to have any daughters.
- What costs nothing is worth nothing.
- What gets measured gets managed.
- What I have, is my father's gift to me. What I do with what I have, is my gift to my father.
- What is everyone's business also has to be someone's business.
- What is the use of running if you are not on the right road.
- What people need and what they want may be very different.
- What the heart thinks, the mouth speaks.
- What we learn from history is that people don't learn from history.
- What we see depends mainly on what we look for.
- When I rest, I rust.
- When it is dark enough, you can see the stars.
- When the tiger kills, the jackal profits.
- When work is a pleasure, life is a joy! When work is a duty, life is a slavery.
- When you act no sin is created and when you react sin is always created, therefore, try to avoid to react and save yourself from committing sin.

Much smoking kills live men and cures dead swine.

- When you buy, use your eyes and your mind, not your ears.
- When you shoot an arrow of truth, dip its point in honey.
- When your hands are tied, your nose itches.
- Where there is dowry there is danger.
- Where there is love there is pain.
- Who offends writes on sand; who is offended, on marble.
- With hardship, there is relief. Eating follows hunger, drinking follows thrust, sleep comes after restlessness, and health takes the place of sickness.
- With money you are dragon, with no money, a worm.
- With more power comes more responsibility.
- Women generally smile when they greet one another but not men!!
- Work related stress and the ills associated with it, are assuming troublesome phenomenon.
- Work will produce more work.
- Years teach us more than books.
- You are a citizen, and citizenship carries responsibilities.

The W.H.O. says the tobacco industry has increasingly directed its marketing campaigns at women and girls. Women currently represent about twenty percent of smokers. But tobacco use among girls is increasing.

- You are unique – none had been like you in the past and none shall be like you in the future.
- You can hold a smile for a long after that it is just teeth.
- You can't make a good deal with a bad person.
- You do not have a problem unless you know it and feel its burden.
- You want to learn from experience but you want to learn from other people's experience when you can.
- Your mind could be your loyal servant as well as your deadliest enemy.
- Your neighbour will never make a boundary fence.

Studies suggest that smoking decreases appetite, but did not conclude that overweight people should smoke or that their health would improve by smoking. This is also a cause of heart disease.

WORDLY WISE : CHANAKYA

- A child beaten by his mother, cries in front of his mother.
- A hungry lion does not eat grass.
- A poor person is even insulted by his wife.
- A small mistake can spoil the whole effort.
- Abusive language destroys the fame of a family tradition.
- Answer should be according to the question.
- Be alert when an enemy behaves well.
- During old age, do not ignore even a small illness.
- Fire has no weakness and electricity too has no mercy.
- Food gives trouble during indigestion.
- Friendship should be extended to an enemy of an enemy.
- Having sex with your maid servant is similar to become her servant.
- Hunger and disease are greater and more powerful than enemies.
- If people do not know what you are doing, they do not know what you are doing wrong.

World No Tobacco Day (WNTD) is observed around the world every year on May 31. It is meant to encourage a 24-hour period of abstinence from all forms of tobacco consumption across the globe.

- It is rare to find a person of innocent nature.
- Man becomes a criminal knowingly.
- Money is the base of all the assignments.
- Never violate the limits.
- No joke while in conference.
- One must save a friend even if he is the son of an enemy.
- People become friends or enemies due to some reason.
- Politeness is grown if we serve old people.
- The calf attacks the udder of his own mother for sucking milk.
- The people of balanced nature are rare.
- The son should be subordinate to his father and obedient to his mother.
- The whole world respect the wealthy.
- There is no dearth of pleasure & pain for the body.
- There is no enemy bigger than one's own pride.
- There is no light like eyes.
- There is no pleasure greater than touching a son.
- Whatever goes to six ears will not remain a secret.
- When anybody says "It's not the money, it's the principle". They mean it's the money.
- Women have hunger two-fold, shyness four fold, daring six-fold, and lust eight-fold as compared to men.

Zero smoking urged on World No Tobacco Day. At last people's movement and implementation of COTPA 2003 effectively across the country in one go (Pulse Time).

Reaching Out & Touching Heart

LISTEN TO MAHATMA GANDHI

A sister said : "I used to pray, but now given it up." I asked: "Why?" She replied: "Because I used to deceive myself." The reply is, no doubt, correct. But let her give up deceiving. Why give up praying?

An eye for eye only ends up making the whole world blind.

An illiterate mother loves her child with her heart.

Believe in Truth, think Truth and live Truth.

Gandhiji attended "Joy Night" in London. A Lady guest asked Gandhiji, "Mr. G. will you also take part in the dance? Where is your dance partner." "Yes," he replied. "I shall certainly dance with my partner - STICK."

If you think of working, your capacity to work will enhance and if you do not think of it, you will lose your capacity.

Laugh like a child (as remarked by C.F. Andrews).

Nobody progresses without opposition.

Nothing can work without rules. The entire solar system would go into pieces if there were even a momentary break of the rules governing it.

The breach of the rule inevitably leads to the breach of other rules.

Tobacco – The silent killer.

The first and foremost service is Latrine-cleaning.

The heart has no language, it speaks to the heart.

The straight path is as difficult as it is simple. Were it not so, all would have followed the straight path only.

Where there is a choice only between violence and cowardice, I would advise violence.

Swami Vivekananda's Winning Formula:

- The world is burning with misery. How can you sleep? Work, Work, Work – let this be your motto. Arise! Awake! And Stop not till the goal is reached.

People with:

(a) Low commitment and low competency. These are like colourless and odourless flowers. They are simple in nature.

(b) High commitment and low competency. These are like colourless flowers but with excellent fragrance.

(c) Low commitment and high competency. These are like flowers with beautiful colours but without fragrance.

(d) High commitment and high competency. These are like flowers with beautiful colours and excellent fragrance.

Life is precious, save it from cancer.

- Faith, faith and faith in yourself.
- When there is a conflict between the heart and the brain, let the heart be followed.
- Full attention, no tension.
- While *Chita* (Pyre) burns a dead body. *Chinta* (worry) burns a living body.
- If you find a hungry man, first give him bread and not teach him religion – this is the true religion.
- Proper diet means simple diet, not highly spiced. Roti is better than *luchi* (Puri).
- Anxiety is worse than a disease.
- The easiest way to make ourselves happy is to see that others are happy.
- Whether you promise to do any work, you must do it exactly at the appointed time, or people lose their faith in you.

Field Marshal K.M. Cariappa – A great man

- It was the year 1965. India and Pakistan were at war. Indian aeroplanes were in action. Some of them were brought down by Pakistan anti-aircraft guns. On the last day of the war, an Indian plane crashed in Pakistan. The pilot was Flying Officer Nanda Cariappa. He was the only son

WHO creates World No Tobacco Day in 1987 observe on May 31.

of the first Indian Commander-in-Chief of free India, (then) General Cariappa. He was captured by the Pakistan army. The then President of Pakistan was Field Marshal Ayub Khan, who had served under Cariappa in the Indian army before independence. Ayub Khan was informed by his officers that General Cariappa's son had been captured. He sent a message to General Cariappa through Radio Pakistan: "Your son is safe. If you so desire I shall set him free." When 66-year-old Cariappa received that message about his only son, he sent his reply: "I will not seek anything for my son which I cannot secure for any Indian soldier. Look after all of them well. They are all my sons."

– K.M. Cariappa

- Cariappa had immense reverence for his parents. Even in extreme old age he used to salute their photographs every morning.

- Cariappa's old age: In 1962 the Chinese army invaded India. The Government of India started recruiting young men to the army. Newspapers in Karnataka carried advertisements asking those who wished to join the army to take an interview on a particular day at a particular hour in a particular office in Bangalore. On the appointed day, there was a long queue. When the officers opened the office and came to the long line they

Do not rub tobacco (khaini) with thumb on your palm. You are destroying your life line.

were taken aback – first in the queue stood the 62-year-old retired Commander-in-Chief of India, General Cariappa!

- A great army officer, a great democrat, a great citizen, and a great man – that sums up Field Marshal Kodendera Madappa Cariappa.

- Learn to obey, then you can command. Learn to be a good 'servant', you can then be a good 'master'.

– K.M. Cariappa

- There is no time to be idle.

– K.M. Cariappa

- Even when people are speaking Hindi, English words keep popping up – Momji and Dadji. It seems such a strange combination of Brit affection and Desi respect. Today young cricketers call Tendulkar Sachin Sir whilst Junior Correspondents call their Boss Rajdeep Sir like Neelu Madam, Rinku Madam, Anand sir, etc. The big poster of coaching centre also projects its teachers in the similar way.

– H.T., Patna, August 3, 2008
Sunday Sentiments – Karan Thapar

- A doctor posted at Rupali PHC (Purnea Distt in Bihar) without performing hernia operation kept the patient for 3 days in his clinic and

A cigarette can only be a perfect killer and nothing else.

administered sleeping inducing drugs. When the patient complained that there was no operation mark in the stomach to the doctor who allegedly told him it was a "*Choomantar*" operation.

– H.T., Patna, March 2, 2011

- DMK leader Annadurai, was one of the best orator in Tamil. He was also well-versed with English Language. Once he was addressing some students. A young student decided to test his mastery over English. He said, "Please Sir, would you compose a sentence in English in which the word 'because' is used thrice consequently." Everybody was upset. Annadurai positioned himself and said, "Ah, my friend that seems to be a very simple question. No sentence can end in 'because', because 'because' is a conjunction." The student lustily cheered Annadurai.

- There is confusion everywhere these days. The judiciary is busy with executive functions, the legislature with investigations and the executive with everything other than governance.

– Former Lok Sabha Speaker, Shri Somnath Chatterjee
– E.T., New Delhi, March 10, 2011

- Whenever my younger brother attends "Reception Party", he always carries two gifts in upper pockets of his shirt. I asked "Why two gifts?"

Cancer can be defeated, if you can leave tobacco before time is out.

He said, "If there is Non-veg then this (higher amount) if Veg (lesser amount) then that." He is strictly Non-vegetarian.

- In Bank, if you hold two posts, two mobiles will be provided to you to look after the work of both the departments but entitlement of 'Personal Entertainment' will be only one.

- A secretary is holding the post of Industries, and also Agriculture. In the morning, he recommends to establish industries at a particular place and in the afternoon when he sits in Agriculture department, he objects that since it is an agricultural land, the industries cannot be erected.

- Suspension is not a punishment, but a reward. An officer made a hectic efforts for his suspension on flimsy ground. In fact, he did not want to go outside the HQ. At last, he was suspended on the ground of rough tongue (Used *Saala*). His life was made comfortable. He was not transferred at a distant place. He engaged himself with traditional agricultural work with family. He was reinstated after a considerable years with full benefits as '*Saala*' is not a *Gali*.

- Bank officer can avail of Festival Advance in a calendar year. He has to mention the name of the Festival. Seeing there is no festival in near future even *Purnamashi* or *Ekadshi*, he mentioned 'Film Festival' as it was going on in the city.

Make no smoking zone.

- Once a Traffic Police checked my Maruti Car. He found that all papers were in order. Then he said, "It appears that it is a new car, that is why everything is available." I felt a sigh of relief though the car was absolutely second hand. I told – yes, yes it is a new car. Then he asked for "Sweets", as it is a new car.

- Quotation of L1 (Lowest-1) provides you other quotations also to procure business without violating rules and regulations by the office. It is difficult to buy the best quality item at the cheapest rate.

- If a Welfare Scheme achieved 100% target silently, it may end up in a whisper or wind up as a racket. If there are no complaints, it may appear that organised corruption is prevailing there.

- We abuse and humiliate people by comparing them with ass, dog, and buffalo. Every human being directly or indirectly depends on animals. They lead a systematic and error free life.

- A lady on the occasion of her Golden Marriage Anniversary said: "When I was married in Assam, the trees were cut down to construct a road. Now after 50 years, the trees were being planted on the roadside."

- When a crow cows, we chase it away. We are afraid that guests may pester us. Though everybody knows Guest is God – *Athithi Devo Bhava*. But,

Curb the cancer menance.

while performing the last rites of our elders, we invite crow. If it accepts our offering, we see our ancestors in the "crow." If not accepted we feel guilty. What is this paradox?

- Complaints about NRIs deserting their wives are sky rocketing. In Punjab alone, at least 20,000 cases are pending against NRI husbands.

- In US Divorce Insurance Wedlock claims to be the first in the world to offer divorce insurance. In India you have the LIC's Jeevan Saathi (for both husband and wife together) or marriage endowment plans (start saving for your daughter's wedding when she is born).

- Children entering school from the next session will not learn the days of the week by their names as we know but by new *avtars* like Wife's Day, Mothers Day, Fathers Day, Thanksgiving Day, Environment Day, Bosses Day, Teacher's day, Women's Day, National Chocolate Ice cream day (US), Thanks giving day, Valentine Day, etc.

- A bank officer asked a customer to produce any sort of identification as per Bank's Rules for instant cash payment of draft (Purchase of the Instrument). Without any hesitation, the customer took out his wallet, extracted a couple of crisp one rupee notes, placed them before the officer with his Index finger pointing to the signature on the notes and asked him whether he was satisfied.

To smoke or not to smoke the decision is entirely yours.

It was then he realised that the gentleman was none other that Shri C. Bhothalingam, I.C.S. and secretary to the Department of Revenue, Ministry of Finance, GOI, New Delhi.

- The forgotten art of shoe throwing has been a dramatic revival. Earlier in more genteel days, shoes were thrown after newly weds for good luck. You must practice the throw several times in advance, because the real idea is not to hit the target, but to just miss them. One size fits (read hits) all and becomes over night matinee Idol. Now, shoe throwing is a global pastime! The *'joota'* is the new weapon of mass disruption. Can there be any business like shoe-business?

- If a account holder of a bank died and his wife requests the bank to transfer the balance amount in her account, the Branch manager will write a letter as under: With reference to your letter dated: ... we shall be glad to receive the Death Certificate of your late husband to enable us to do the needful in the matter. The Branch Manager's letter surprised and the lady was in dismay. The lady barged into BM'S chamber the very next day and threw the letter on BM'S face and started abusing him. She shouted, "Instead of feeling sad at the untimely death of my husband and sympathising with me, you wrote - you would be glad to receive his Death Certificate? What harm had he done to you? And as if that was not enough, the parting kick was. If something

Smoking reduces the women's fertility.

would happen to your wife tomorrow, will you be similarly glad?" The BM replied calmly, "Madam, you have not met my wife. If you had known her, you would not have asked this question."

- Always do innovative and creative things. When I was Branch Manager in Madhupur, I organised "*Aao Rachaein Mehndi.*" I invited the lady Superintendent of Police (S.P.). The entire Madhupurwasi thronged to see her. It was a grand success.

- Depression would be the most dreaded disease after heart attack by 2020, if it is not curbed. It is caused by a sense of haplessness, helplessness and worthlessness. The remedy lies in changing the mind. There is no joy in committing suicide.

- A woman was sweeping at the wee hours at Heathrow Airport. I asked, "Who is your supervisor?" She replied, "If I have a supervisor, then the supervisor will have his own supervisor. So there will be hats off supervisor for one work i.e. sweeping."

- Once an Incoming and Outgoing DGM visited my branch together. I welcomed our new DGM by saying enthusiastically that Sir, it is a Red letter Day for us. The outgoing DGM was so furious and asked me over the phone – was my tenure a Black letter day? Sorry sir, 'noted for future'.

- Some of the world's most lasting literary works including fiction, autobiography, poetry and philosophy – were written or attempted to begin

Hello, "do cellphones cause cancer?"
WHO focusing on environmental and life style factors that may contribute to cancer.

while their authors were in prison.

- Many people who constantly complaint that they forget names, they don't really forget them. Actually, they never remember them in first place. As a matter of fact, sometimes they never ever hear them.

- It is all in the stars – Noida's Marigold Public School has invited astrologers to counsel students based on their horoscopes. It can help map out a student's strengths and weaknesses, and to select courses most suited for success. Stop worrying and start living it up.

- There was no women actress in India's feature film– "*Raja Harischandra.*" All the female characters were played by men in the early years of Indian cinemas.

- A friend of mine was crazy about 'foreign goods'. He could not think high of anything 'Indian'. One day he visited a doctor's clinic and complained severe pain in his eyes. The Doctor examined him and said, "You have exactly what you like most, a 'foreign particle' (material) is there on your eyeball. Well! Would you like to remove it, or would you prefer to keep it?"

- I praise Goddess Lakshmi 'Mother', if you kindly allow me to have Rs. 1 lakh by way of reward for my devotion to you, I promise to donate half of it at

Eat fresh vegetables. Use fully vitamin 'A' and 'C' to control weight.

one of your temples. But if you have doubt in my word, then straightaway deduct Rs. 50,000 and give me the rest.

- Some people turn to God. Some turn to alcohol. Honestly speaking, I don't see any difference. Both ways life is being guided by a Spirit.
- We are afraid of living as well as dying. Living is not the same as making a life. The manner of your living will dictate the manner of your dying. Life is to live, let live and forgive.
- Rambola was married at the age of 14 with a beautiful Ratnavali whose charm rendered him her slave. Once she said, "If you have such devotion to me why not devote to GOD." This changed his life from Rambola to Tulsidas.
- Wherever you go, you go without prejudice. We all have seen the puppy and monkey playing together. Puppy is very small and nascent to his new world. He does not have any mindset about monkey. Both puppy and monkey enjoy each other. Once puppy knows about monkey activities, he must not dare to mix with monkey.
- Once a guide showed the dotted line to Pandit Jawaharlal Nehru and his team. They said, "Nothing is visible, even dotted line." Then the guide said, "It is visible only to those who have devotion to God." Everybody claimed – "It is visible, it is visible."

Change your life style to protect from cancer.

- The Sun, it can be only appreciated, by its absence. The longer days of rain and cold, the more the Sun is craved. But too many hot days, and the Sun overwhelms. However, in the beginning make yourself not scarce but omnipresent. Absence create respect and esteem. If presence diminishes fame, absence auguments it.

- When more customers visit a business centre, the businessman feels extremely happy to receive "*Paikar*" but in bank it became the talk of the Drawing Room.

- India is the largest English speaking nation in the world.

- Whenever the Election commission announces its programe for holding election to the Lok Sabha or State Assemblies, paid holidays are declared. When the First General Election was held in the country for Parliament/Assemblies, time off was given to employees to cast their vote without causing loss of working time.

- When Stalin died, Pandit Jawaharlal Nehru made a mention of his death, adjourned the Parliament and declared a public holiday but in USSR of which he was the Leader had not declared a holiday at all. Similarly, when John F. Kennedy was shot dead by an assassin, US observed only two hour

Self-examination of breast at regular intervals is a very highly recommended procedure to detect any alteration in the breast at the early stage. Not all lumps are cancerous cancer.

recess for his funeral. In India, you know better. Even the government takes time to decide whether or not to declare a holiday, on sudden death of a leader. Delay in making the declaration leads to resentment and claim for overtime.

- In no other country in the world, the number of holidays are more than India. A peculiar tradition – schools, colleges and offices are closed one day before the actual festival in the name of "Shobha Yatra". Holiday is declared to pay homage or celebrate birthday of a prominent personality.

- British Empire, with all-out efforts, could not even force one per cent men to wear neck-tie but today in free India, girls are forced to wear it because it is a school uniform.

- Shri Hanuman went to Lanka, found Sita and came back. He did the reporting with two words. "*drista* Sita" meaning seen Sita. These days reports run into thousand pages or may be in 18 chapters, on such a situation with endless conclusion.

- William Weds Kate: Britain's William places the wedding ring on the finger of his long-time girlfriend Kate Middleton in front of the Archbishop of Canterbury Rowan Williams at Westminster Abbey, London, on Friday, 29th April, 2011. They were pronounced husband and wife as they exchanged vows with two simple words "I will."

Excess food, leisure, liquor and hormonal changes cause breast cancer, says experts

- Baffled by Mahatma Gandhi's strategy of non-violence, an English collector sent his Telegram to the Secretariat: Kindly wire instructions on how to win a tiger non-violently.

- The wind becomes friendly with the fire that burns the woods. But the same wind extinguishes the fire in a small lamp. Who will be friendly with the poor? The suggestion is to be strong enough to stand "On One's Own feet."

- People like the result of *Punya* or Merit, but never like the result of *Paap* or Demerit. People do not like the results of *Paap* or Sin, but commit the sins knowingly, with effort.

– Subhashita Ratnavli, January 14, 1989

- The problem of managing the Boss has stayed with the mankind since time immemorial. And it is totally unlikely to disappear in the near future. Hating the Boss is no solution, it does not solve any problem. The best solution however, lies in making the Boss say "What do we do in this case or what do you suggest?" After making the matter complex by you.

- When any fashion becomes current, many would follow it without any judgment as to its propriety or importance. Tendency of imitation is prevailing in men.

World Cancer Day, 4th February and World Health Day, 7th April.

- There is an erroneous notion regarding the motion of the sun who has, broadly speaking, no motion and still erroneously believed by all of us that the sun rises in the east and sets in west. It is also true in human nature.

- Once a poet was reciting a couplet and claiming that it was his own couplet. Then his fellow poet at the *mehfil* questioned that the particular couplet was of Mirza Ghalib. Then he said, "*Hamare Khayalaat unse milte hain.*" I wondered, "*Cycle Aur Hawai Jahaj Ke Ek Se Khayalaat Hotein Hain.*"

- There are two kinds of people in this world:

    1. Those who remember names.

    2. Those whose names are remembered in this world. Choice is yours.

- Our Foreign Minister SM Krishna has been the butt of jokes for reading the Portuguese Foreign Minister's speech in the United Nation instead of his own setting out our government's position. However, he observed, "These things do happen." Actually they do. It happened in a case in England before the celebrated Judge Lord Eldon. The Solicitor General in his opening speech argued with gusto all the submissions of the opposite side. When the court brought this to his notice, the unflappable

SG said, "My Lords, I have fairly argued all the points which could be urged by the other side. I shall now demolish each of them."

– The Indian Express New Delhi, February 27, 2011

- A Heart full of Burden : What T.N. Seshan beautifully says in the following golden words:

  (a) I have a heart full of burden. That is called India.

  (b) There is one-half of the population which is oppressed, depressed, suppressed, compressed. They are called women. First Suraksha then Arakshan.

  (c) *Kaka* Joginder Singh aka Dhartipakad wanted to establish a record of the maximum number of defeats he has had.

  (d) Nobody dies twice.

  (e) There is a law in this country for every purpose.

I am told by some Judges of the Supreme Court that the per capita availability of laws in the world is nowhere as high as it is in India. And implementation of them is nowhere as deficient as in India. But, none of these gets implemented and the rest of the population of the country lives happily ever after.

- What a sad commentary on our culture and civilisation? A cow is well-fed because it gives milk but the child is neglected. Whereas no investment is more profitable than investment on child.

- You have said some good words about me. I do not know if you really know me and my qualities. There are many things which appear on the surface but they are really not so, in substance. If I look good and innocent to you, you should not mean that I am not a clever man. I would not say, a cunning man.

– Lal Bahadur Shastri: Speech at the meeting of women's organisations in Hyderabad on March 21,1965

- Entire India is running on "certificate". Once a borrower asked the Branch Manager to write off his loan account financed under Government Sponsored Scheme (GSS). 'Impossible,' BM shouted. Then the borrower asked under what circumstances it could be waived. Annoyedly the BM told, "When the poorest of the poor borrower died. Oh! On death it could be done." Next day, he brought his "Death certificate" and requested the BM to keep promise for waiver of loan amount. The BM wondered and asked him to bring his "Death Certificate" and then his desire would be fulfilled.

- Ask your father to send false Express Telegram with a serious tone so that leave may be granted

Tobacco kills, don't be duped.
Cancer is not contagious or infectious.

without demur by the tight Boss. But this is no "moral" for both father and son.

- Ramanujam fell seriously ill in 1917 and his doctors feared he would die. He was on his bed in a London hospital, when G.H. Hardy visited him. Hardy told Ramanujam casually, "I came over in cab number 1729. That seems a rather dull number to me." "Oh, no!" Ramanujan shot back. "1729 is the smallest number you can write as the sum of two cubes, in two different ways." It is 103 + 93 = 1729 or 123 + 13 = 1729

While Phrases : What they mean!

Under Consideration	We have lost the file.
Under Active Consideration	We are trying to find the file.
Note and initial	Spreading the responsibility.
Implement the programme	Increase the staff and make the job bigger.
For your immediate action	Do it now or we will get into trouble.
Copy to	Here is a share of headache.
Action is being taken	Your correspondence is lost and we are still trying to locate it.
For your necessary action	It is your headache now.

Cancer is reluctant to provide you a second chance.

For your information, please	I will not do anything on this.
We had a free and frank discussion	We exchanged discussion allegations.
Useful discussion	Only talked.
Officer was sober today	He is a habitual drunkard.
During a strike	No business was transacted as usual.
Lawyer	If the Lawyer wins the case for the client, he will lose a client.
Bicket checker	Checks for personal monetary gains.
He is taking rest	The Boss is sleeping.
Is boss on "Tour"	The Boss is on 'trip'.
He has been officially elsewhere	The Boss is late.
He purchases Sundry Items	If he purchases T.V. Remote Control, Flower Vas etc.
If an employee makes a mistake	It is a mistake.
If our Boss makes a mistake	It is our mistake.
If a barber makes a mistake	It is a new style.
When I take a long time	I am slow.

United for a tobacco free world and not tobacco world.

When my Boss takes a long time	He is thorough.
When I don't do it	I am lazy.
When my Boss doesn't do it	He is too busy.
When I do something without being told	I am trying to be smart.
When my Boss does the same	That is initiative.
When my Boss pleases his Boss	He's co-operating.
When I do good	My Boss never remembers.
When I do wrong	He never forgets.

- A meeting was called in to pray for rain. Many gathered for prayer. But a small boy came with an umbrella. That is the real faith in the power of prayer.

- Faith is the first condition of success. Sri Ram neither tested Vibhishan nor expressed any doubt on him rather imposed faith on him and got success.

- The Foreign newspaper respected Alfred Noble as the death of the dynamite king and merchant of death.

- Mr. Nasruddeen Amarjit, Publisher, Illustrator and Calligrapher handed over the first copy of his

Sport and art without tobacco: Play it tobacco free.

book (Rs. 1200) to Khuswant Singh "as a gift". "It will not be a gift. It will be your first sale," said Khushwant Singh firmly and thrust the notes (Rs. 1200) in his hands.

- Looking at a sunset, just for a second you forget your separateness: you are the sunset. That is the moment you feel the beauty of it. But the moment you say that it is a beautiful sunset, you are no longer feeling it, you have come back to your separate, enclosed entity of the ego. Now the mind is speaking. And this is one of the mysteries, that the mind can speak, and knows nothing, and the heart knows everything, and cannot speak, perhaps to know too much makes it difficult to speak, the mind knows so little, it is possible for it to speak.

  – *Osho Quotes*

- During course of our examination, a student asked Einstein, "Sir, all these questions are the same as in last year's papers!" Einstein grinned and said, "But the answers will be different."

- Alexander Graham Bell died on August 2, 1922. On the day of his burial all telephone services in the U.S. stopped for one minute in his honour.

- "If you say only your strong points, you may lose the case. Tell me your weak points also, so that

Tobacco free workplace : Safer and healthier.

I may tamper it efficiently, as usual, to protect your case," said the lawyer to his client.

- When I was posted as Regional Manager, the local print media (newspaper) printed my Bio data under the head 'Who is He' instead of 'Who is Who'.

- It is estimated that 3000 pages or 250 million words are being printed every minute at the global level. The growth rate of book publication is roughly three times greater than global population growth.

  – THE HINDU Speaks – May 7, 1996

- Gautam Buddha was referred to as "Light of Asia" in the poem written by Edwin Arnold.

- 11.11.11 good day for divorce too – Mumbai : As droves of couples queued up at the marriage registrar's office on Friday to read their sacred vows, barely a kilometre away in Bandra, the family court too was abuzz with activity. The court received 32 applications on 11.11.11 from warring couples seeking, among other things, divorce, maintenance or protection from domestic violence – THE TIMES OF INDIA, SATURDAY, NOVEMBER 12, 2011.

- DELHI–CONFEDENTIAL : SEATING PROBLEMS: The Fifth SAARC Conference of Speakers and Parliamentarians in New Delhi posed a tricky problem for Lok Sabha Speakerr Meira Kumar. Faced with an embarrassing number of empty

The word "Cancer" comes form the Latin word 'Carcinoma' meaning crab.

seats in Central Hall, she could have opted for an adjournment for lack of quorum had it been an ordinary session of Parliament. However, this being the inaugural ceremony of the SAARC event, she obviously did not have that option. She had to look for some other quick-fix solution, so the staff of the Lok Sabha were promptly parked among the audience to save the day for their boss – The Indian EXPRESS, New Delhi, Monday, July 11, 2011.

- MOON WALK : Gujrat Chief Minister Narendra Modi was keen to meet US astronaut Neil Armstrong who was the first person to steo on the moon. Mr. Armstrong spoke to him with immense warmth. During the meeting, Mr. Modi asked him if he can summarise his experience in two sentences and what he said then remains etched in my memory. Mr. Armstrong said, "When I went to the moon, I went as an astronaut and when I came back, I came as a human being. This is my realisation, Modi wrote – The Indian EXPRESS, NEW DELHI TUESDAY, AUGUST. 28, 2012.

- CYCLE CULTURE : Justice Dalveer Bhandari is to leave for the Hague next month (June 2012) to join the International Court of Justice. Bhandari was perplexed when he received a phone call from Hague asking whether he would like a bicycle to be booked for him. In India, Justices are used to limousines and pilot cars and the thought that in the Hague, most people travel by cycles for short distances came as culture shock to the honourable judge – The Indian EXPRESS, New Delhi, Sunday, May 20, 2012.

One Tobacco Many Troubles.
Many cancers are caused by habits, customs and usages.

- Out of print : Those weighty tomes that once seemed to hold within them the entire breadth of human knowledge will be no more – Encyclopaedia Britannica will cease publication after 244 years to concentrate solely on its online product, a sign of the times, if there ever was one – The Indian EXPRESS, NEW DELHI, FRIDAY MARCH 16, 2012.

- The Encyclopaedia Britannica will of course, continue to dispense through website, in an obvious nod to the spirit of the age. The Encyclopaedia, once the pride of libraries and an ideal of responsible if affluent parenting, held sway as long as information was structured and stolid, and mostly flowed from Anglophone countries to the rest of the world – HINDUSTAN TIMES, PATNA, FRIDAY, MARCH 16, 2012.

BLUNT TALK'S IN FASHION, INDIA!

- SPIT-FULL : The Bombay High Court said last week "Spitting is an inherent character of our people", while hearing a petition about people being fined for spitting in Mumbai. A few days later, it was revealed that in just six months in 2011, Mumbaikars had paid around Rs.2.24 crores in fines for spitting in the city. Well, as long as the inherent character makes us some money.

- Press Council of India chairman Justice (retired) Markandey Katju, said on Saturday, the 24th March, 2012 that "90% of people in India are fools. Their minds are full of superstitions, communalism and casteism. They elected

Phoolan Devi to Parliament since she belonged to a backward caste. He was speaking at the convocation of Bharatiya Vidya Bhavan Sardar Patel College of Communications & Management.

- In March, 2012 Greg Chappel, former Team India coach said that "The (Indians) culture is very different. They lack leaders because they are not trained to be leaders. From an early age their parents make all the decisions. They learn to not take responsibility". Now, now aren't our men famous for listening to momma? – THE TIMES OF INDIA, PATNA, SUNDAY, APRIL 1, 2012.

- 'Cow' resolution leaves Punjab House staff in a fix : Chandigarh, August 24, 2012 : AFTER the Punjab Assembly made an obituary reference to cows, allegedly slaughtered a bone crushing factory at Joga village in Mansa district, the Vidhan Sabha staff is in quandary over whom to send the formal condolence message.

- As per normal practice, condolence resolutions adopted in the Assembly are normally sent to the next of kin of all those are paid tributes during the obituary references at the opening of each Assembly session. Chief Minister Parkash Singh Badal later also declared that a memorial would be set up for the slaughtered cows. The project is likely to cost around Rs. 2 crore – The Indian EXPRESS, New Delhi, Saturday, August 25, 2012.

There is no safe level of exposure to second hand smoke.

- MY LIFE IS MY WORK : Swami Ranganathananda
- When you go to a Hindu merchant to collect the promised amount, you will be greeted often with the words : come tomorrow. This will rarely happen in the case of the Burmese Buddhists merchant. He makes you feel you are wanted and gives you the promised amount with a sense of devotion.
- I remember reading it in the papers, when Sardar Vallabhbhai Patel was arguing a case in the court, a man delivered a telegram to him. He just read it, put it in his pocket, continued his arguments and then went home, to see his dead wife. That was the telegram. How many of us can withstand that shock calmly? It is not for want of love, love was there. But something more was there : the capacity to withstand the ups and downs of life.
- Wherever I go in India, the first question I often ask of people when they are introduced to me is: "How are you?" To this I often get the answer: *Jaisa Chalta Hai* – somehow is going on.
- 'Kitchen cloth – dirtiest things in Indian homes'

  The kitchen cloth used in most Indian households is highly contaminated with bacteria that have the potential of causing food-prone diseases, a study has found.

Your dreams of lighting up in a public place have just gone up in smoke.

- Shockingly, the study by the Global Hygiene Council found kitchen cloths to be dirtiest items in homes.
- About 95% of kitchen taps failed the hygiene test, making it the second dirtiest item in the households.
- Contaminations were found on 92% chopping boards and knives.
- "It should be washed at high temperatures or disinfected regularly to break the chain of infection" said Professor John Oxford, Chairman, Hygiene Council and Professor of Virology at Queen Mary College, University of London - Hindustan Times, Patna. Monday, October 01, 2012.

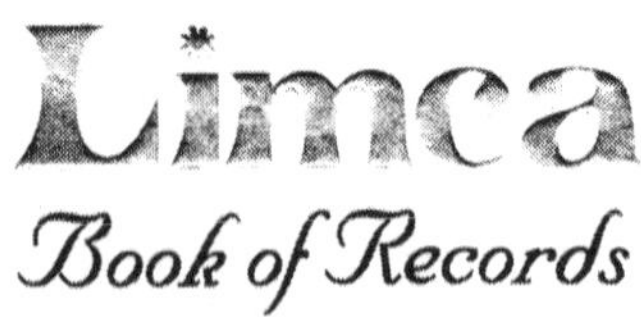

National Record 2013

Naresh Chandra Mathur (b Jan 12, 1951) of Patna, Bihar published Punchline in Jan 2012 containing pithy sayings of great women and men with 1112 quotes. Brought out by Pustak Mahal, what special is in the one-liner cancer awareness slogans at the bottom of each page, a unique way to spread the message!

Vijaya Ghose

Make

every day

World No

Tobacco Day.